Adventures in the Justice Factory

Courtroom Tales of a Notoriously Unreliable Witness

Matthew Mendenhall

ISBN: 978-1-7344559-1-5 Paperback
ISBN: 978-1-7344559-5-3 Hardcover
ISBN: 978-1-7344559-0-8 eBook

Cover Design by: Cover Creator.
Library of Congress Control Number:
Printed in the United States of America

Dedication

For my parents, Robert William Mendenhall and Jenne Anne Mendenhall. For my wife, Linda Anne Little, and our daughters, Sara and Amy, all of whom carefully read the manuscript of this book and made numerous corrections and excellent suggestions. For my siblings, Rachel, Mark, Peter, Maria, and Robin Mendenhall. For Nana (Jenne Knapp-McCarty) and Uncle Mark McCarty and all of the branches of our family, far too numerous and broad for the entire assembly to fit comfortably inside a single circus tent. For all of us who are still here, and all of us who are long gone but not forgotten. For Ms. Jane Ball, a fine high school English teacher who told me long ago that she hoped I would write a book one day. For a long, long line of inspired teachers, kind colleagues, true friends, and splendid acquaintances.

For all of the dedicated people with whom I worked at the United States District Courts for the Southern District of California—judges, courtroom and support staff, administration, and probation and pretrial services officers. As admirable as our system of justice is, it is far from perfect. Over the years, I saw that things didn't always work out for the best in every single case. For whatever reason, justice would somehow get lost in the shuffle. Whenever this happened, however, it was never due to a lack of commitment or due diligence on the part of the many outstanding people who comprise the aforementioned organization. I have been gone for a number of years now, but my hat is still off to all of you, and it always will be.

And for my fellow court interpreters who, day in and day out, quietly scale yet another Tower of Babel. Climbing syllable by syllable, at times drained and exhausted, you reach the members-only top floor an amazing percentage of the time. Nobody ever said it was going to be easy, but oh interpreter, for you alone, the view from the top! So, you didn't quite reach the heights today? Never fear, you will tomorrow. So, you aren't perfect after all? Bah! Perfection for interpreters is measured in unintelligible milliseconds. These stories are for you, with admiration, many thanks, and fond regards. In other words, love.

CONTENTS

Preface

Stories and memories … memories and stories. There being no time like the present, what better time is there to recount my adventures in the "justice factory?" Might it not be more accurate to say, "There being no time *but* the present, what *other* time could there be to recount my adventures in the "justice factory?"

Regardless, the criminal cases and anecdotes recounted in these stories are real. All of them took place over a period of years in the courtrooms or environs of the United States District Courts for the Southern District of California, located in San Diego, California. I worked in the federal courts in San Diego as a federally certified, Spanish-English court interpreter, first on a freelance basis, then on staff for a little over twenty-five years, from 1985–2010. The Southern District of California comprises San Diego and Imperial Counties, both of which border Mexico. The criminal conduct described in each story occurred in one or the other of these counties.

Court interpreters serve the courts by interpreting the proceedings conducted in English in the courtroom (and oftentimes outside the courtroom as well) into the native language of defendants, witnesses, and other participants in criminal cases who are not sufficiently fluent in the English language to be able to understand and meaningfully participate in the proceedings. In like manner, court interpreters interpret the language spoken by non-English-speaking defendants, witnesses, and other participants into English for the court, attorneys and the jury throughout all phases of criminal proceedings, including jury trials and sentencings.

Court interpreters are neutral officers of the court. We swear an oath to interpret and translate the proceedings in all matters in which we serve accurately and faithfully to the best of our abilities. While working within the adversarial context of our legal system, court interpreters are ethically bound to remain impartial at all times. Our allegiance is always to the court. Thus, while the role of court interpreters is to facilitate clear, accurate communication between the court, the prosecution and the defense, court interpreters are not on the side of the prosecution or the defense. We share the same workspace with the prosecution and the defense, but we have no stake whatsoever in the cases for which we provide expert language services, nor any interest in their final outcomes. If we have any opinion about any matter in which we serve, we keep it to ourselves. Our job duties and position of neutrality give us a unique vantage point from which to observe the myriad matters that come before the courts.

A number of years passed between when these cases were heard in court and when I wrote the stories that they inspired. As a result, some of the facts pertaining to each case made a wild break for freedom and escaped the confines of my memory entirely. Still other facts closely resembling donkeys seem to have snuck off when nobody was watching, only to reappear years later, mysteriously transformed into great American bison, shaggy long johns and all. In other words, all of the stories (with the exception of "Court Suggestion Box") are factual in origin, but "fictionalized" in the telling. Mark Twain is credited for saying, "Never let the truth get in the way of a good story." I have long since forgotten the names of the defendants whose cases I've recreated in these stories. Nevertheless, I have used fictitious surnames for the defendants where necessary, not so much to protect the innocent as to respect the guilty. I have also used fictitious surnames for other participants as necessary.

How were these experiences "adventures?" What I mean is, were they really adventures, or did I just happen to be there doing my job, and so witnessed and/or took part in them? They were definitely not adventurous in the same way as catching a big tuna at sea, although if you think about it, where else would one catch a big tuna or a small tuna or *any* tuna for that matter, if not at sea? Still, if one does not pin "at sea" on the tail of the phrase, the image hangs there somehow incomplete, as though a huge shark had bitten off the whole tail end of the fish, leaving little but the head behind, to dangle sadly on one's line …

Nevertheless, they were surely "adventures" in some sense of the word, perhaps in the same way that a waterlogged swimwear catalog washed up on a remote island shore might conjure up a skimpy string of "adventures" to a lonely castaway, if only in the meager cupboards of the imagination.

What's the difference if they were real adventures anyway? The title has a grandiloquent, ridiculous ring to it, reminiscent of a few masterpieces of bombastic oration I interpreted over the years. Let those who read these lines decide what sorts of tales herein reside.

Stories and memories… memories and stories…

1. The Singing Bicycle Bank Robber

"Just as you sometimes catch one small blue fin tuna when you least expect it, mixed in with a huge school of albacore, so you sometimes encounter an innocent defendant when you least expect it, mixed in with a huge school of guilty ones. It doesn't happen very often, but it does happen, believe it or not. Just as you release the stray tuna because it's too small, so you release the stray defendant because he's innocent. Let him go! Throw him back in the ocean and let him live to swim another day!" (from the author's journals)

Many years have passed, but I still recall an unusual case of a singing bicycle bank robber. He was a Mexican defendant charged with bank robbery in federal court in the United States of America who needed the services of a Spanish-language interpreter, which explains why we interpreters were assigned to his trial. For as far back as any of the interpreters could remember, of all the bank robberies allegedly committed by Spanish-surnamed defendants, he was the *only* one who had ever used the services of the interpreter throughout the proceedings. Also, in marked contrast to many other defendants for whom we routinely found ourselves interpreting in court, this particular defendant used the services of the interpreter because he genuinely needed to do so. In this regard, the defendant was an exception to a curious rule: if you want to rob a bank in this country, you had better be able to speak a little English. Otherwise, how do you get your demands across to the teller?

Regrettably, a couple of fierce grunts and menacing gestures would seem sufficient to accomplish the task. I suppose that a would-be robber more attuned to the daunting challenges of intercultural communication might consider engaging the services of an unwitting interpreter to convey his demands to the bank teller. Needless to say, there would be no legal requirement that a certified interpreter be hired for such deplorable engagements.

The fact that the defendant used his beat-up, old bicycle as the getaway vehicle was another of the unusual aspects of the case. During the trial, we watched the two of them on the bank's security videotape—the Mexican defendant pedaling the bike, and his alleged accomplice—a young American woman—draped awkwardly on the handlebars. After the heist, he exited the bank first, then got on his bike and started pedaling away. Seconds later, his female accomplice came out of the bank and evidently hailed her "getaway driver." He paused for her to hop onto the handlebars again. Then off they went, only to crash in an alleyway a short distance away. Or so he said in his testimony at trial.

Another curious thing the defendant said during his testimony was that he was not in the least bit guilty of robbing the bank with "that American lady." According to the defendant, what he *was* guilty of doing was having sold her a small amount of heroin for seventy dollars, but that was not the crime with which he had been charged. He testified that if they had charged him with selling the heroin, he would have pled guilty and taken his punishment like a man. Unfortunately, they accused him of bank robbery and of aiding and abetting bank robbery. Consequently, as the defendant went on to explain, he felt compelled to go to trial as a matter of principle, seeing as how he was not guilty of those particular charges and should not be punished for something he had not done.

To hear the defendant tell it, the bank robbery was a completely unintended event resulting from a misunderstanding—a misunderstanding that, in turn, arose out of a chance encounter between speakers of different languages. He was a fieldworker in the Imperial Valley and had no immigration document that permitted him to be in the United States legally. Hooked on heroin himself, the defendant was sharing an apartment with various other fieldworkers and was selling small amounts of heroin to support his own habit.

He finished work one day, returned home, and rode his bike to a convenience store to buy two quart-sized bottles of beer—one for himself and one for a friend back at his apartment. In the store parking lot, he crossed paths with a young American woman who had just walked away from a voluntary stay at a drug rehabilitation facility located across the street. She too was addicted to heroin, and her mother had paid for an inpatient treatment program for her. After having spent a couple of very uncomfortable days of sobriety, she could no longer withstand the withdrawal symptoms, and had left. She was shaking and nauseous, looking for a fix, and had no form of payment in her purse except for a credit card.

Arrested herself shortly after the incident and later indicted for bank robbery, the young American woman had signed a plea agreement with the federal prosecutor and had pled guilty to one count of bank robbery. As part of her plea agreement, she had agreed to cooperate with the federal prosecutor and to testify against her alleged accomplice at his trial, which she did. In exchange for her truthful testimony, she hoped that the federal prosecutor would recommend to the court that she receive a more lenient sentence.

During the trial of her Mexican codefendant, the woman testified that she initially approached him outside the convenience store to ask if he knew where she might get a fix. According to her, the young Mexican male seemed to understand English well enough to be able to negotiate a drug deal with her. He agreed to sell her a small amount of heroin for seventy dollars. She testified that once the young Mexican understood that she did not have cash on hand to pay for the heroin, it was he who suggested the idea of robbing the bank as a means for her to get cash to pay him for the drugs.

In contrast, the Mexican defendant testified that he had understood that the young woman did not have cash to pay him for the heroin, but what he had tried to convey to her was that they could go to the bank, and she could use her credit card to get cash to complete their transaction.

The Mexican defendant testified that after this initial conversation, he rode his bicycle back to the apartment to take the beer to his friend. While at the apartment, he also picked up the heroin that he sold to the young American woman afterward. When he came back to the convenience store parking lot, she was there waiting for him. There was some further garbled exchange between them, then off they went to the bank. As it was a hot day, and the bank was a few blocks away, he offered her a ride on the handlebars of the bicycle. She accepted his offer and hopped aboard. According to the Mexican defendant's sworn trial testimony, he had no idea that the young American woman was planning to rob the bank.

Once at the bank, he parked the bike and followed her inside. According to the testimony of an assistant manager at the bank who witnessed the robbery, the woman walked to one of the tables where customers fill out their transaction forms. There, she picked up a form and wrote something on it. The assistant manager testified that while the woman was standing at the table writing something, the man stood next to her and spoke to her. The woman appeared to be talking to him also. The assistant manager was seated across the lobby from the two "customers" standing at the table. She was unable to hear what they were saying. Nevertheless, it appeared to her that while the male spoke to the female, he was also looking at the paper on which she was writing, as though he were telling her what to write.

The woman testified that she finished writing out the demand note and got in line, followed by her alleged accomplice. The two of them waited briefly, until the next available teller called to them. They approached the teller, and the woman handed the note to the teller without saying a word. The note had been hastily scribbled in English. It said something to the effect of: "This is a robbery. Give me all your cash." The teller testified that she smiled at the woman, then looked at the note. For some reason, the teller did not immediately understand the note. She testified that her first thought when she looked at it was that these two "customers" had come inside from the automatic teller machine located outside. The machine had been behaving erratically that day, and some customers had been having problems with it. Then the teller looked at the woman again and noticed that she was not smiling back at her. The teller looked at the note more closely, and she also stopped smiling. Hands trembling, she emptied the cash from her drawer and handed it to the woman, who then turned and walked quickly toward the door. Her "accomplice" had already started walking ahead of her and was sitting astride his bike by the time she got outside.

As I recall, there was a spirited debate among the interpreters about the Mexican defendant's role at this juncture in the chain of events, and about how we should best refer to him. The purists, cleaving closely to the classic jargon of bank robbery, smugly pronounced that the Mexican defendant was the "wheelman," and that was that. But was he? If, as the two of them lurched clumsily along the hot streets of that desert town, the defendant had it in his mind to make a quick, clean getaway from the bank that they had just robbed, then he was indeed a "wheelman," so to speak. But others, focusing on his more rudimentary mode of conveyance, reasoned that it was more accurate and perhaps less confusing to call him the "handlebars man." Still others, focusing on the fact that his female accomplice was seated on the handlebars while he was both grasping them and also pedaling the bike, argued quite reasonably that it would be more precise to refer to him as the "auxiliary handlebars man," or perhaps the "primary pedal man." After going "around and around the mulberry bush" to no avail, a consensus was ultimately reached that it didn't matter a hill of beans how we referred to his role among ourselves, so long as we interpreted all of the trial proceedings faithfully and accurately.

During the trial, after the "pedal man" completed his direct examination, the prosecutor cross-examined him at length. In response to the prosecutor's questions, the defendant testified that he remembered that the young woman had gone inside the bank first, and that he had followed her to the table where she had written something on a slip of paper, which he could not see, much less read. Moreover, as he spoke little English and the woman did not speak Spanish, he had no idea that she intended to present a demand note to the teller. Then, during the defendant's testimony on cross-examination, in a brief lull between one question and the next, there came a seemingly unrehearsed moment of unusual candor or inspired mendacity, as the case may be. It was as though the defendant had remembered something important and needed to blurt it out to the jury.

"Oh, I wanted to tell you something," he said. "When the lady from the bank came here yesterday and testified, she said that she saw me talking to the young lady. The thing is that I wasn't talking to her."

"You weren't talking to her?" asked the prosecutor.

"No, I was singing," answered the defendant.

"You were *singing*?" asked the prosecutor incredulously.

"Yes, I was singing."

"What were you singing?" asked the prosecutor.

"'Vuelve Conmigo,'" ("Come Back to Me"), replied the defendant.

"'Come Back to Me?'" repeated the prosecutor.

"Yes," replied the "pedal man."

For a fellow on trial for such serious charges, the Mexican defendant was surprisingly at ease throughout his time on the witness stand. He appeared unflappable, despite the many thrusts and jabs of the prosecutor's rigorous cross-examination. The defendant went on to recount how he and the American woman had ridden the bike into an alley a short distance away from the bank. There they had lost their balance and toppled over. No one was badly hurt, but the woman was sick and had started throwing up. She paid him seventy dollars, and he handed her the heroin. He testified that he didn't know how much money she had gotten from the teller, because it was her transaction and none of his business.

According to him, that was the reason why he had started walking away from the teller window before the teller had handed the money over to the woman. Once their heroin deal was complete, he got back on his bike and rode off down the alley. The last he saw of her was when she had paused to throw up again as she walked along.

Minutes later, officers of the local police department, who had heard the broadcast of the Mexican defendant's description over the radio and had spotted him riding his bicycle along the street, stopped the defendant and arrested him. Meanwhile, his accomplice had stopped at a house along the alley. There she asked for permission to use the telephone and called a taxi. The taxi arrived and picked her up. At her request, the taxi headed directly toward Mexico. Before the taxi reached its destination, however, units of the local police managed to intercept the vehicle, after which the police arrested the female passenger. Among her scant belongings, the police recovered over $2,000 in cash. As for the "pedal man," when the police booked him and inventoried his belongings, they recovered a whopping seventy dollars.

In the end, was the defendant a knowing participant in a bank robbery, or was he a small-time heroin dealer who got played for a chump by a desperate addict? We'll never know for sure, but the members of the jury only took a couple of hours to reach their own unanimous conclusion and acquit him of both charges. I was interpreting for the defendant when the verdict was returned. One should not read too much into these small gestures, but when I interpreted the words "not guilty" as to each count, I noticed that the defendant did not react in any of the ways I have sometimes seen other defendants react when they are acquitted by juries. He did not bury his head in his arms, thank God effusively, or burst out sobbing in relief. In fact, he hardly reacted at all, except to nod his head slightly in agreement, almost as though he had expected it all along.

2. "Too-Non-Doo"

Four of us were crowded around a table in a visiting room in the downtown federal jail: the probation officer, the defendant, his defense attorney, and me—the interpreter. The defendant had already pled guilty and was awaiting his sentencing. The probation officer was interviewing the defendant pursuant to an order by the court that the Probation Office conduct a presentence investigation of the case and prepare an extensive presentence report for the court. A weak sun filtered into the room through the narrow window in the corner, and the hollow space reverberated with an overlapping hubbub of many voices, as several legal visits were in progress at the same time.

The defense lawyer was doing her best to prompt her tight-lipped client. "Go ahead and tell the probation officer about the witch doctor," she cajoled him once again. I interpreted what his lawyer had said into Spanish for the defendant. He just leaned back in his chair, smiled a huge, embarrassed smile and shook his head. I remember thinking that he was a remarkably happy man for being stuck in jail thousands of miles from his native Colombia and facing maritime cocaine-smuggling charges that exposed him to a potential life sentence. Maybe poor fishermen are happy by nature. Or maybe happiness is one of the few basic necessities that a poor fisherman can afford. One thing seemed very clear: happiness costs a whole lot less than cocaine.

The defense attorney addressed herself to the probation officer. "I don't recall any mention of this in the reports of investigation, but there is something I wanted my client to tell you," she said. Then she turned back to the defendant and prodded him again. "Go on, tell the probation officer about what happened with the witch doctor before you left Colombia," she said. "The probation officer needs to know how you and the other four men came to be out on the ocean on that 'go-fast' boat, so that she can recommend an appropriate sentence to the judge in your case. Tell her what it was that you and the other members of the crew were chanting over and over again while the coast guard boarding team approached your boat."

I interpreted what his lawyer said to the defendant, and he smiled again. "If I tell her, do you think that it will help me with my sentencing?" he asked.

"I don't know if it will help, but I'm pretty sure that it won't hurt you either," his attorney replied with an encouraging smile.

The defendant smiled back at his attorney. "OK," he said. "Before we left Colombia, we went to the witch doctor in our town to ask him for protection on our voyage north to deliver our cargo and return safely home. All five of us pooled our money to pay the witch doctor for a magical charm to keep us safe on the journey. The witch doctor took our money. He told us that if we were to find ourselves in danger of being detected by the United States Navy ships, all we had to do was to chant 'Too-Non-Doo,' 'Too-Non-Doo,' over and over. A big, thick fog bank would appear by magic. The navy ships would not be able to find us in the fog, and in that way, we would escape, finish our journey and return home safe to Colombia."

"So, the whole crew paid the witch doctor for a magic charm, which was supposed to protect you from being discovered and boarded by the coast guard?" asked the probation officer. "What does 'Too-Non-Doo' mean?"

The defendant smiled sheepishly and said, "I don't know what it means. Supposedly, they are magical words that you say over and over again to ward off danger. As you can see, they don't work very well."

"So, once you saw the coast guard cutter approaching your boat, what happened?" asked the probation officer.

"At first, we kept going, because we weren't sure if they had seen us. Then, all of a sudden, a helicopter flew over the top of us, and someone was shouting something at us, but we couldn't hear what they were saying because of the noise from the helicopter and from our motors. We just kept on going. Then we heard shots, and we saw bullets hitting the water in front of our boat. We were all very scared, and we kept on going. Then we heard more shots coming from the helicopter, and the bullets hit our motors, and the motors stopped working, and we stopped."

"What did you and the other crew members do then?" asked the probation officer.

"When the motors shut off, our boat was just drifting. We all started praying and chanting 'Too-Non-Doo,' over and over. Then a small boat approached our boat. There were sailors in it, and they were pointing guns at us. An officer told us in Spanish to keep our hands up, and to go and sit in the bow of our boat. So that is how they boarded our boat and arrested us."

"So, no fog bank appeared?" asked the probation officer.

"No, no fog bank appeared," the defendant replied sadly.

"Tell the probation officer about the other boat that was going to leave Colombia at the same time as your boat," prompted his attorney.

"Oh." The defendant smiled ruefully and shook his head once again. "There was another boat, and another crew of fishermen from our town. They were supposed to embark at the same time and make the journey with us. The captain of that boat believed that the witch doctor was charging too much money for protection for their journey, so he refused to pay him. Then the rest of the crew got scared and refused to go on the trip."

The probation officer finished writing her notes of the defendant's account and looked up at him. A hint of a smile flickered across her face. "Let me see if I understand you, sir. You are saying that the crew of your boat paid the witch doctor for magical protection, and then you embarked on your journey. After several days at sea, the coast guard boarded your boat. All of you were arrested, despite having paid the witch doctor for magical protection from danger, and despite the whole crew chanting this 'Too-Non-Do' over and over while the coast guard boat was approaching your boat. Meanwhile, there was another boat that was supposed to make the journey along with your boat. That boat had a stingy captain who refused to pay the witch doctor the going rate for magical protection. Because of that captain's refusal to pay the witch doctor, his crew got scared and refused to make the journey. Consequently, the other boat did not embark at the same time as your boat, and so that crew did not get boarded and arrested. Is that what happened?"

I finished interpreting what the probation officer had said to the defendant. He smiled yet again and nodded yes. Then he mumbled something that I did not understand, so I said, "Excuse me?" to him.

"Goddamned witch doctor!" said the defendant, plenty loud enough for me to hear. Then he shook his head and laughed heartily, and for just a moment, his laughter drowned out all the sadness in the room.

3. "They Can't Make Me Go to Trial!"

Many years have passed since this alien smuggling case was heard by the court, but for a long time afterward, whenever my fellow interpreter and I bumped into one another, we would invariably recall the luckless defendant who they forced to go to trial against his will, and we would laugh once again. I am embarrassed to say that I laughed at the defendant's expense—that is, at his seemingly hapless lot in life. I describe him as hapless despite the fact that the evidence against him was overwhelming, and that he had stubbornly denied his guilt until the very last minute.

The defendant's lawyer had reviewed the facts of the defendant's case with him, had explored possible defenses, and had laid out his options. Based on his review of the evidence, and exercising his sound professional judgment, the defendant's lawyer had repeatedly advised the defendant to accept a plea agreement and resolve his case by pleading guilty. As he had explained to the defendant, if he chose to resolve his case via a negotiated plea agreement, it was highly likely that he would ultimately be sentenced to serve substantially less time in custody than the three-year mandatory minimum sentence that he would receive if he were to be convicted of the charges against him at trial. Disgruntled with his lawyer's unvarnished advice and counsel, the defendant steadfastly refused to take the deal. In fact, on the morning of the first day of trial, he expressed his general dissatisfaction with the performance of his court-appointed lawyer and asked the court to relieve his lawyer and appoint another one to represent him. Because the defendant's request was last minute, and also because he gave no compelling reason for wanting another attorney, the court denied the request. (This business of defendants "shopping" for a different court-appointed lawyer until they find one that suits them sometimes brings to mind a jostling crowd of bargain hunters pawing through racks of suits placed on clearance at a men's discount clothing store.)

Our obstinate defendant has long since served his time, been deported to Mexico, and is well beyond earshot. Even so, one should never laugh at another's misfortune, and I confess that I laughed anyway. But I also laughed at his righteous indignation about being compelled to go to trial when he ultimately had no wish to do so. Indeed, he tried his best to plead guilty on the morning of trial, to no avail.

For our part, we were just as puzzled as he was about the situation. I mean, why not let the defendant plead guilty? Why make him go to trial after he had stated to the judge repeatedly under oath that he was guilty of engaging in the same criminal conduct as two other defendants who were arrested with him, and whose guilty pleas the judge had just taken and accepted in his presence? Nevertheless, as the interpreters assigned to that case or to any case, we are not like those picky judges at a gymnastics competition. It is not our job to rate on a scale from one to ten the comparative sense or senselessness of the events that unfold before our eyes and ears in court.

He was a defendant in a large-scale, alien smuggling conspiracy involving multiple defendants. Alien smuggling as a commercial criminal enterprise is the business of cross-border trafficking in human cargo. It entails the organized, illegal crossing of undocumented foreign nationals into the United States from abroad for purposes of making a buck, and ultimately delivering the human "cargo" to its destination, preferably undetected by officers of what was formerly known as the United States Immigration and Naturalization Service.

Our defendant was one of several foot guides/drivers employed by the ring. The job of the guides was to lead groups of undocumented immigrants on foot through the rugged mountainous terrain of southeastern San Diego County to prearranged places along the roads and highways, where vehicles would be left for their use. The group would remain hidden in the brush until their guide would give them the signal, whereupon they would scamper out from their hiding place and pile into the car as fast as possible. Three or four aliens would hide and travel in the trunk, while the rest of the "load" would ride in the passenger compartment. The guide would then take the wheel and drive the load vehicle to one of the so-called "drop houses" used by the smuggling organization. The guides/drivers employed by the ring were also undocumented immigrants. If stopped by the Border Patrol, the driver would oftentimes attempt to pass himself off as just another member of the group, in hopes of being quickly processed and returned to Mexico along with the rest of the detainees. Once the undocumented passengers were safely stashed at the drop houses, they would be harbored for varying periods of time, then loaded into vehicles and transported northward to Los Angeles or to wherever their ultimate destination might be within the United States.

For several months prior to the defendant's arrest, a team of Border Patrol agents had been assigned to investigate alien smuggling activities in the eastern part of San Diego County. Over a period of approximately thirty days, this unusually thorough team of criminal investigators had observed, videotaped, and meticulously documented the method of operation of the particular alien smuggling organization for which our defendant was employed. The anti-smuggling team's investigation ultimately led to the detention of more than twenty undocumented immigrants as well as the arrest and prosecution of a half dozen individuals. In addition, the government seized a number of vehicles along with one or two houses that had been used to harbor the undocumented immigrants. Most of the seized vehicles and real properties belonged to two siblings who were two of the three main defendants in the case. The siblings ended up going to trial along with one of the guides who had been their employee.

Border Patrol agents detained our defendant at one of the ring's drop houses, together with all of the other undocumented immigrants whom he had just delivered to the house. The surveillance agents observed that the defendant, upon arriving at the drop house, looked around, opened the trunk of the car, then quickly escorted all of the occupants of the vehicle to the door of the house. In addition to their own observations, they arrested the defendant because several of the smuggled passengers, upon being questioned after their detention, positively identified the defendant as the person who had guided them across the border and through the hills to the pickup point along the highway. They further identified the defendant as the person who had then driven them to the house. The defendant, along with one of his fellow guides, also made an exuberant attempt to flee from the agents when they approached him at the house, but that may have been the least compelling piece of the government's evidence against him.

By the time the first day of trial arrived, one of the six defendants—perhaps the "biggest fish" of the group—had already pled guilty. Five defendants—the two siblings and the three guides—were scheduled to go to trial. After the abovementioned hemming and hawing about changing attorneys had concluded, and prior to the start of jury selection, the attorneys for all three of the guides informed the court that their clients had recently experienced a change of heart, and that now each of them earnestly desired to plead guilty.

(The following lengthy digression seeks to explain why it struck the trial interpreters as so peculiar to see a seemingly run-of-the-mill defendant being compelled to go to trial against his will. By way of background, around the time this trial was held in the mid-to-late 1990s, things were a little different in the courts than they are now. In those days, we also had very high numbers of criminal cases but fewer judges to preside over them. Working in our courts was like working in a luxurious cattle chute with top-quality padding on the posts, gates, and rails. It was like a highly decorous, state-of-the-art production plant where hundreds—sometimes even thousands—of units of "finished justice" were assembled and shipped out per annum. Drug smuggling cases, alien smuggling cases, and illegal entry cases were our three main "model lines." Reacting as best they could to an unending stream of criminal cases, the courts had morphed into a mass-production environment. Time mattered. Indeed, time mattered so much that many of the judges resorted to handling routine criminal proceedings in groups, including the taking of guilty pleas en masse from defendants in completely unrelated cases. We also had numerous jury trials involving the same kinds of charges over and over. Each trial takes time, effort, and money, and the judges only had so much time.

Interestingly enough, no one seemed terribly troubled by the "cattle herd" brand of justice that we found ourselves practicing. Perhaps people realized that desperate times call for desperate measures. Nevertheless, there were occasional mix-ups. For example, due to the marshals endlessly escorting back and forth huge numbers of in-custody defendants—many of whom shared the same or similar-sounding names, and all of whom were similarly clad in jail-issue jumpsuits—the wrong defendant would occasionally be brought before the court. In such cases, fortunately not very often, the defendant himself might not realize the mistake in time, or he might lack the presence of mind or intestinal fortitude to communicate to the court that he was not the defendant whose case and name had been called by the court clerk. Thankfully, other defendants seemed to have a curious sense of pride about the relative prestige of their charges. These defendants would pipe up indignantly if they heard themselves being mistakenly referred to as alien smugglers, when they were in fact drug smugglers.

On top of this, if a case was called and the wrong defendant was brought before the court, and at the same time the lawyer representing the defendant did not recognize his or her client by sight, then a thick, bewildering fog of confusion and error might settle over the proceedings—if not on the spot, then later on. This same sort of head-scratching mix-up of defendants could also happen if a lawyer stood in for the attorney-of-record for a single court appearance. Having never met the defendant, this luckless lawyer making the so-called "special appearance" would occasionally forget to verify that the defendant who had been brought before the court was in fact the "right" person. As a result, the "wrong" defendant might go through an entire phase of another defendant's court case without anybody discovering the mistake until afterward, if at all. When I think back to those days, I'm amazed that there were as few foul-ups as there were.

With so many defendants passing through the "plant," there were also abundant numbers of recidivists, or "repeat customers." Needless to say, each and every one of our "customers"—first timers and repeat offenders—represented an essential unit of "raw material" for the "justice factory." Regrettably, many repeat offenders, instead of humbly embracing the rigorous honesty of rehabilitation, quickly learned to lie and finagle their way through the system. Consequently, problems resulting from the widespread use of false names and birth dates were to a certain extent inevitable. On one occasion, a judge finished imposing sentence on a repeat offender. As the marshals were leading the defendant out of the courtroom, a sudden inspiration lit the judge's face.

"Hold on a minute, Mr. So-and-So," said the judge. "Let me give you a piece of advice. The next time you are arrested, be sure to write down on the back of your hand the name you give to the agents. Whatever you do, remember that name. We've had prisoners who forget the name that they gave the arresting agents, so once they are booked into the jail, they never answer when the jailers call them out for court. We've had prisoners lost in jail for months because they can't remember their name!" The defendant nodded gratefully as the marshals led him away.

Of course, one cannot entirely discount the possibility that a few smart alecks have slipped through the system over the years, thinking what an inspired bit of tomfoolery it would be to answer when the marshals called out a name similar to their own. If their mischief went undetected, they could easily wreak havoc on the case of the unsuspecting defendant whose name they had temporarily assumed. Moreover, given the tens of thousands of defendants processed through the courts over the years, it is not inconceivable that at least a few defendants have pled guilty to the wrong charges, whether by confusion, error, hapless bumbling, or some inscrutable twist of fate.

Small wonder then, that no sooner were the words out of an attorney's mouth that his or her hitherto trial-bound client suddenly wished to plead guilty, than the courts would make all reasonable and dignified efforts to accommodate the defendant's wish before he might be stricken with the first debilitating pangs of "buyer's remorse." All defendants in criminal cases have a constitutionally guaranteed right to a jury trial. Nobody—especially not the court or court staff—must ever do or say anything to influence or curtail the defendant's personal choice to exercise his right to go to trial. The court, along with all court personnel, must never do or say anything that might in any way be construed as a preference that the defendant—however strong the evidence may appear to be against him—settle his case by pleading guilty rather than going to trial. Therefore, out of respect and by necessity, court staff always keeps a poker face in the solemn environs of the courtroom. But once outside, as one inhales the fresh air of the real world, how sweet it is!

"What did you say? The defendant has pled guilty? So, that trial has gone away after all? Oh, happy day!" The only thing approaching that rush of elation was when the court would ever-so-reluctantly agree to a last-minute continuance of a trial.

Don't get me wrong: at no time did I ever see any attorney "bum-rush" or bamboozle a defendant into pleading guilty. Over the years, I do recall a couple of occasions when attorneys, while advising their clients to "take a deal and plead out," made what sounded to me like sentencing-related "promises" to their clients—promises that the attorneys did not have the power or authority to keep. Curiously, on this same topic of inducing defendants to plead guilty, I once had the occasion to translate a handwritten, signed agreement between two codefendants who were in jail together while awaiting trial on charges of marijuana smuggling. By means of this neatly drawn, rather formal contract, defendant A bound himself to pay a large sum of money to the wife of defendant B in exchange for defendant B's taking the fall for the marijuana and exonerating defendant A. The idea was that defendant B's wife would need a substantial pile of cash to see her through the lean times while her husband was serving his prison sentence. Unfortunately for the two codefendants, prison staff intercepted their contract before they could close the deal.

It goes without saying that no one ever rolled out a red carpet in the courtroom or ordered up fine cigars and expensive champagne in grateful appreciation of a defendant's guilty plea. By the same token, the courts were never so accommodating as when an attorney needed time, then more time, and then maybe a little more time in court to review a plea bargain with a defendant prior to him entering his guilty plea—especially on the eve or morning of trial.

I think at least some of us who worked in the courts daily saw little purpose in a given case going to trial if the defendant was in fact guilty as charged, and if he was ready, willing, and able to plead guilty. It seemed eminently sensible to allow the defendant to plead guilty, provided that he did so freely, knowingly and voluntarily. If a jury trial happened to be scheduled on a morning when the defendant changed his plea from not guilty to guilty, and a jury panel had already been summoned, then the judge would simply send the group of prospective jurors back to the jury room to await further instructions. When this happened, I for one was thankful that we did not have to go through the time and effort of yet another trial.)

As the trial was about to begin, and the time for the defendants' acceptance of a plea agreement had long since passed, the three guides had no bargaining leverage at all. Their only option, if they wished to plead guilty, was to plead guilty to all of the charges in the indictment, of which there were more than a dozen. This was not a big problem for the defendants, as they would be sentenced to concurrent time on all of the charges and would thus be exposed to the mandatory minimum sentence of thirty-six months in custody. So, the court had the clerk administer the oath to the three defendants and proceeded to take their guilty pleas. Because the defendants were all pleading guilty to the same charges, and for purposes of efficiency, the court addressed its advisements and questions to all three of the defendants throughout the plea colloquy, and the defendants answered in turn.

Then it came time for each of the defendants to provide the so-called "factual basis" for their guilty pleas. The three defendants had all been sitting and standing next to one another throughout the guilty plea colloquy with the court, in ready earshot of everything said by the court, their lawyers, and their codefendants. The court posed a series of questions to each of the defendants individually in order to determine that they were in fact guilty of all of the counts relating to the three main charges in the indictment: conspiracy to bring in and transport undocumented aliens, bringing in undocumented aliens, and transportation of undocumented aliens.

Each of the defendants admitted that he had committed numerous specific acts that very clearly established that: 1) they were members of a criminal agreement or partnership (i.e., a "conspiracy") to smuggle undocumented aliens into the United States from abroad; 2) on the specific dates alleged in the indictment, they had brought (i.e., "smuggled") undocumented aliens into the United States; and 3) on those same dates, they had transported undocumented aliens in the United States.

After questioning the first and second defendants, the court asked the prosecutors if they were satisfied with the factual basis provided by each defendant. Without hesitation, the prosecutors responded that they were satisfied. The court then posed the same series of questions to the third defendant. With minimal coaching and counsel from his attorney, the third defendant admitted that he had committed the same series of criminal acts as his two codefendants.

Then the court asked the prosecutors if they were satisfied with the factual basis provided by the third defendant. As far as we could tell, there were no substantial differences at all between the facts admitted by each of the three defendants. As a result, we were a bit taken aback when the prosecutors responded that they were not satisfied with the third defendant's factual basis.

As I recall, there were a couple of huddled conferences between the court and the lawyers, after which the court would again question the defendant as to the facts underlying his guilty plea. If memory serves, during at least one of these conferences, the court spoke only with the prosecutors, which seemed slightly out of the ordinary. Each time the court questioned him, the defendant would again state clearly and unequivocally for the record the facts that made him guilty of each of the counts in which he was named. In all, the defendant made several attempts to plead guilty, and each time, for some unstated reason, the prosecutors were unsatisfied with his plea. In the end, despite the defense attorney's token protests and the court's signs of displeasure with the prosecutors' unyielding stance, the court acquiesced to the prosecutors' wishes and refused to accept the defendant's guilty plea.

As the hearing progressed, the defendant's reactions also progressed. Like a proud peacock gradually spreading its magnificent fan, the defendant was surprised, then confused, then stunned, and finally indignant. He was a poorly educated man, unschooled in the vapid verbosity of federal criminal procedure, but he was no fool. Soon enough, he grasped the import of what was happening. When he heard my interpretation into Spanish of the prosecutor's final statement to the court that the government was not satisfied with his factual basis, he asked his attorney, "Does this mean they won't let me plead guilty?" His lawyer asked the court for an opportunity to consult with his client, which the court granted. The defendant's lawyer was by no means a well-heeled barrister and could undoubtedly make very good use of the considerable additional income that he would earn by representing his client throughout a lengthy jury trial. He looked at the defendant with a curious mixture of pity and elation.

"Yes, that's right, Mr. Carrillo," he told him. "They are not accepting your guilty plea."

"Why not?" asked the defendant. "I'm just as guilty as the other guys. Why can't I plead guilty?"

"I know you are," replied his attorney. "But as you have heard, the prosecutors are not satisfied with the factual basis of your plea, and because of that, the judge will not accept your guilty plea."

The defendant thought for a second, then asked his attorney, "If they don't let me plead guilty, does that mean that I have to go to trial?"

"Yes," answered his attorney. "You have to go to trial."

The defendant shook his head adamantly. "But I've already pled guilty, and I don't want to go to trial," he said.

"I know you don't, but you have no choice," said his attorney.

The defendant's features hardened, and he set his jaw. "They can't make me go to trial!" he scoffed. "I want to talk to the judge."

"What do you want to say to the judge?" asked his attorney.

"I want to ask her why they won't let me plead guilty."

The defendant then addressed the judge. "Your Honor, I don't want to go to trial," he said. "I have already pleaded guilty, and I am just as guilty as the other guys."

The judge looked at the defendant sadly and addressed him in a voice that seemed to drip with caring and compassion. "Mr. Carrillo, I understand that you do not want to go to trial, and that you have stated to me under oath that you are guilty, but the prosecutors are not satisfied with the factual basis of your plea, and so I cannot accept your plea."

"So, does this mean that I have to go to trial, even if I don't want to?" asked the defendant.

"Yes," replied the judge.

"They can't make me go to trial!" scoffed the defendant.

"Mr. Carrillo, I know that this is very hard for you," the judge explained to the defendant in that same empathy-laden tone of voice. "But in fact, since I have not accepted your guilty plea, the truth is that you *do* have to go to trial. In fact, we are going to start the process of jury selection as soon as the panel of prospective jurors arrives."

The defendant shook his head. "No, no. This is not right," he said. "They can't make me go to trial!"

But that, as it happened, is exactly what "they" did. Before the panel of prospective jurors arrived, the defendant's lawyer explained to the defendant that during the evidentiary phase of the trial he would not be presenting an affirmative defense, because the defendant had already pled guilty. Nor would he be rigorously cross-examining the prosecution's witnesses against him, because they were not really disputing the charges. He also explained to the defendant that during the trial, all he had to do was sit at the defense table and listen to the proceedings, and that at the end of the trial it was highly likely that the jury would find him guilty. With arms crossed, the defendant listened stone-faced to his lawyer's explanations. From time to time, he would shake his head, as though to dispel the idea that any of it applied to him. His features hardened into a stern frown of disapproval, a frown that remained on his face throughout the trial, which lasted for several days.

As best he could, the defense attorney sought to mollify the defendant by assuring him that he was not going to be punished more harshly for having gone to trial. He explained to the defendant that the court understood that he had admitted his guilt under oath and had already accepted his responsibility. Therefore, the attorney had every confidence that the defendant was not going to receive a stiffer sentence for going to trial and being convicted by jury verdict than he would have received if the court had accepted his guilty plea. Either way, given the peculiar posture of his case, the defendant was going to receive the mandatory minimum sentence of three years. The defendant, however, was in no mood to be mollified.

"So, if I am going to get the same sentence either way, why do I have to go to trial?" he asked, but the attorney was unable to give him a satisfactory answer.

For the first couple of days during the trial, when the marshals would bring the defendants out from the holding cells in the morning and seat them at the defense table, the defense attorney would cheerfully ask the defendant how he was doing. Without so much as a glance at his attorney, the defendant would either reply, "Badly," or "Very badly," depending on how he was feeling that morning. After a day or two of trying to humor the defendant a little bit, or cajole him out of his stony silence, the defense attorney gave up. After that, their attorney-client communications shrank to a few pitiful crumbs of unilateral civility such as "Good morning, Mr. Carrillo," or "I'll see you after lunch."

True to his word, the defense attorney devoted almost no time at all during the trial to cross-examining witnesses, making objections, or presenting arguments. And just as he had predicted, the jury speedily convicted the defendant of every count in which he was named in the indictment. Finally, true to the defense attorney's prophecy, the defendant was ultimately sentenced to the mandatory minimum of three years in federal prison—exactly the same sentence that his two fellow guides received from the court.

So, when all was said and done, why did the defendant have to go to trial? Did the defense attorney engage in some gamesmanship, or perhaps lamely attempt to extract unacceptable concessions from the government during those last-minute bench conferences held on the first morning of trial? Assuming that was not the case, why did the prosecutors want the defendant to be present in the courtroom along with his other two remaining codefendants? Did they fear that his more powerful codefendants had somehow threatened or intimidated him, and that he might try to "fall on his sword," so to speak, and make some sweeping proclamation to the jury that his codefendants had nothing to do with the crimes? Did the prosecutors want him to be present as a representative guide/driver, in order to be able to present to the jury a more complete and compelling picture of the role played in the alien smuggling conspiracy by the guides/drivers, and to perhaps shed light on the connections between them and the operators of the drop houses? In their righteous zeal to obtain convictions against all of the defendants, were the prosecutors merely intent on portraying the despicable subject of commercial trafficking in human cargo in the most damning light possible? I will never know the answers to these questions, and my purpose is not to second-guess the defense, nor to cast stones at the strategy of the prosecution. The defense attorney knew perfectly well what he was doing. The prosecutors were well-prepared, seasoned, ethical practitioners, and they must have had their reasons.

Still, whatever those reasons were, it has always seemed to us that by virtue of being compelled to go to trial against his will, the defendant found himself reduced in stature to little more than a "tackling dummy" for the prosecution. He was like a guinea pig that was not even afforded the basic dignity of refusing to venture out of its tiny cage in the morning if it didn't feel like it. No wonder he never veered from his course of stern, stoical silence throughout the trial. Thinking about it, although I don't speak a single word of guinea pig, I would have been unhappy too.

4. “God Bless Crooks!”

The marshals, court security officer, and I were sitting in court one morning, waiting for the judge to come out from his chambers and take the bench. The conversation rolled around to “crooks”—a term which law enforcement personnel often use to refer to “the accused” or “the defendant” when court is not in session.

Our court security officer (CSO) that morning was a gruff ex-cop who walked with the ambling gait of a bear. Powerfully built, instinctively suspicious, vigilant and kind, he had put on too much weight for his own good, and he knew it. Old age was catching up with him, pushing back his hairline, and turning his bushy mustache gray. Retirement from a long, full career at the police department had left him with a pension. He was blessed with reasonably good health, a loving wife and family. After a brief stab at retirement, he had gone back to work as a court security officer.

As we were sitting there talking, someone made a disparaging remark about crooks. I don’t remember who it was, but I do recall what the old CSO replied.

“People bad-mouth crooks all the time, but hey, stop and think about it,” he said. “Without crooks, where would we be? Probably every one of us would be out of a job. God bless crooks! I made a good living off of them for thirty years!”

It may be that his remark stopped the conversation in its tracks, or there may have been a few noncommittal nods and grunts of assent. I recall that I smiled at him and nodded in agreement. The conversation ended shortly afterward when the judge came out and took the bench.

As the court clerk called the cases on the calendar, the marshals quietly and efficiently went about their job of escorting prisoners in and out of the courtroom. I positioned myself at the entrance to the jury box and interpreted the proceedings for the Spanish-speaking defendants as their cases were called and heard. As for the CSO, he took his seat next to the courtroom doors. For a few minutes, his bespectacled eyes watched every move the defendants made. Gradually, as the proceedings droned on, he leaned back in his chair, laced his fingers across his midsection, and rested his head against the elegant wood paneling behind him. Soon, his eyes began to glaze over, and his head started to nod. Slowly but surely, he settled into a pleasant, late-morning nap.

A few years after that routine morning in court, he retired for good. A few years after *that*, I heard from another CSO that the old officer had died. I think maybe his heart gave out. It's a funny thing, but if you stop and think about it, he may have been right about crooks.

Rest in peace, old policeman, and never fear. Day in and day out, there continues to be a steady supply of crooks out there committing crimes, getting arrested, and being hauled into court. There are more than enough crooks to keep the "justice factory" operating at peak capacity until the last gavel falls. "God bless crooks!"

5. Roy Bean

Similar to a fly diving headlong into a Venus flytrap, there are many pitfalls lurking in the courtroom, just waiting for the unsuspecting court interpreter to blunder into unawares. Luckily for court interpreters, when we stumble into a pitfall, there is at least one vitally important difference between our fate and the fate of the luckless fly. Sooner or later, we get to buzz our way back out of the sticky heart of the flytrap, while the fly generally gets stuck there for the duration of the proceedings. Such a pitfall was the unmitigated fiasco of "Roy Bean."

One day, the telephone rang in the interpreters' office. It was getting close to the noon hour, and I was sitting in the office by myself. When I answered the telephone, it was one of the court clerks calling on behalf of her district court judge. The clerk whispered urgently that there was a witness on the stand who needed an interpreter. I said that I would be right there and hung up the telephone. I checked the assignment schedule and saw that nobody was assigned to cover that court. Scribbling a brief note for the supervising interpreter, I grabbed my notebook, dictionary, and pen, and headed for court. I walked as fast as I could to the elevators, took the next car up one floor, and walked fast to the courtroom.

Pushing open the door, I noticed a courtroom full of faces, many of whom turned to look at me as I entered. The judge was on the bench, while his court clerk and shorthand reporter sat at their places in front of him. The jury box was full of jurors and alternate jurors, and the prosecution's table was crowded with prosecutors and agents. The defense tables had been expanded to fit a sizable school of defendants and their lawyers, and the gallery at the back of the courtroom was full of onlookers. I also noticed a very large man with a beard sitting at the witness stand. A number of strategically placed marshals rounded out the scene.

I nodded and said, "Good morning, Your Honor," as I walked past the podium and approached the witness stand. There I stopped and waited. The judge said, "Good morning, Mr. Interpreter. Thank you for coming. Madame Clerk, will you please administer the oath to the interpreter?" The court clerk duly administered the interpreter's oath to me, whereby I ceremoniously raised my right hand and solemnly swore to accurately and faithfully interpret English into Spanish and Spanish into English to the best of my abilities, so help me God. All of the interpreters already had an oath on file with the Clerk's Office, but many of the judges would still have us sworn in for the record when we were called upon to interpret for witnesses at the stand, particularly when there was a jury present.

I then put my dictionary down at the marshal's bench and took up my position next to the steps at the foot of the witness stand. I had time to notice once again that the witness was a very large man—so large that he barely fit in his seat. I nodded to him and stood with my notebook and pen at the ready, waiting for the attorney to begin his cross-examination.

"Mr. Torres," began the attorney, "I'd like to ask you a few questions about Homero Troyano."

"OK," replied the witness, and I noticed that he spoke with a rolling, rumbling voice that seemed to originate from somewhere deep down in the bowels of a volcano.

"Where did you meet Homero Troyano?" asked the attorney.

"Yo lo conocí en un 'Roy Bean,'" is what I heard the witness reply in that deep, rumbling voice. I had never heard of "Roy Bean" before and hadn't the slightest idea who or what "Roy Bean" might be. Nevertheless, based on the name itself, in that split second before I interpreted his answer into English for the court and jury, it struck me that "Roy Bean" was likely the name of a steakhouse or else a country-western bar. Therefore, I confidently interpreted the witness's reply into English as: "I met him at a Roy Bean," then waited calmly for the attorney's next question.

The attorney looked down at his notes with a puzzled expression, and then looked up at the witness again.

"Mr. Torres, did you say that you met Homero Troyano at a Roy Bean?" he asked. I interpreted his question into Spanish for the witness.

"Sí, en un Roy Bean," replied the witness, and I interpreted his answer as, "Yes, at a Roy Bean."

The attorney looked even more puzzled and asked the witness, "Mr. Torres, who or what is 'Roy Bean?'" I interpreted the question into Spanish for the witness. To my surprise, the witness rolled his eyes upward, shook his head, smiled broadly, and leaned down from the witness stand toward me. *"¡Lo conocí en un 'droy-veen!' ¡En un 'droy-veen!'"* he said more emphatically, addressing only me.

For a second, I looked up at him in a state of utter incomprehension, my lips silently forming the words that he had just spoken. Then the light dawned on me, and I felt like the biggest fool in the phone book. A bottomless chasm of embarrassment yawned before me. The only thing that flashed through my mind was to try somehow to convey to the court and jury that I had never seen this witness before in my life. So, I looked up at the witness, smiled sheepishly, and nodded my head vigorously up and down, as if to say, "Oh, *now* I get it!" like the last person to get a very obvious joke at a party. The witness nodded his gigantic head at me and smiled sympathetically. My face and ears were flushing red as I interpreted his correction of my ridiculous mistake into English for the court and jury: "I met him at a *drive-in*! At a *drive-in*!"

Everyone in the courtroom burst out laughing and they kept on laughing. The judge was laughing; the court staff was laughing; the jury was laughing; the defense lawyers and defendants were laughing; the prosecutors and agents were laughing; the marshals were laughing; the spectators were laughing, and the gargantuan man perched like Humpty Dumpty on the witness stand was also shaking with laughter. The only person who was not doubled over laughing in the courtroom was me. I felt like a man standing stark-naked on the pitcher's mound in Yankee Stadium, wanting desperately to salvage my dignity with whatever came to hand—a dictionary, a notebook, a pen—anything! As much as I love to laugh, I resisted the urge to look around at all those laughing people, like a comedian well satisfied with his punch line. Go ahead and laugh, I thought to myself. If it weren't for me, you wouldn't have any reason to laugh! I looked down at the floor and shook my head ruefully. Then, as the laughter gradually subsided, I stood there and looked at the examining attorney, waiting for his next question.

Before the attorney could serve up his next question, however, the judge addressed the jury. "Well, on that note, ladies and gentlemen," he said, as another wave of snickering broke and rolled through the courtroom, "we are going to take our noonday recess." The judge reminded the jury to bear in mind his previous admonition not to discuss the case and excused the jurors for lunch. Then he admonished the witness to return to court for the afternoon session. I interpreted the judge's warning to the witness. As soon as the judge stood up to leave the bench, I beat a hasty retreat from the courtroom, with my tail tucked between my legs.

Days later, while getting onto the elevator, I bumped into the judge in whose courtroom I had mistaken "drive-in" for "Roy Bean." I took the opportunity to apologize for my mistake. To my relief, the judge smiled and said, "That is the least of my problems."

Oddly enough, after all these years, I realize that Roy Bean taught me a number of invaluable lessons as an interpreter—lessons I might never have had the opportunity to learn if not for Roy's fleeting, hideously humiliating passage through my professional life. Lesson number one: my ridiculous misinterpretation of "Roy Bean" taught me that "flying by the seat of one's pants" is "no way to run a railroad." Interpreters should never be thrown into the situation of interpreting for a witness in evidentiary hearings without the opportunity to speak with the witness beforehand, lest they inadvertently commit mistakes that can affect the outcome of a case. Lesson number two: Roy taught me that as an interpreter I am only as good as what I hear. In other words, sometimes I don't hear what I think I hear, and other times I don't think I hear what I really do hear. Lesson number three: Roy Bean taught me that as a general rule, one is much better off never answering the telephone at all. If and when you must answer the phone, by all means do your level best to disguise your voice.

Finally, Roy Bean may hold yet another, far greater lesson for me—namely, perhaps I should do myself a big favor and abandon thinking entirely. Although, if you think about it, "Roy Bean" *would* make a fabulous name for a steakhouse or a country-western bar, wouldn't it?

6. "Who?"

A deputy marshal recounted this incident to me one afternoon while we were sitting in court, waiting for the judge to come out and take the bench. Like a number of his fellow deputy marshals, this marshal had begun his career in law enforcement working for the United States Border Patrol. As a Border Patrol agent, he had occasionally responded to calls made to the Border Patrol by other law enforcement agencies, such as units of the local police departments and the state highway patrol.

In years past, it was not uncommon for officers of these agencies to stop vehicles for traffic violations and discover that the driver did not speak English and did not have any identification documents, including a driver's license. Back then, if the officers suspected that the driver and the other occupants of the vehicle might be in the United States illegally, they would routinely detain the vehicle's occupants until the U.S. Border Patrol could arrive on the scene and check the immigration status of the driver and passengers.

It was while he was responding to such a call that the deputy marshal—then a Border Patrol agent—had heard a highway patrol officer describe how he had been patrolling a stretch of freeway one day.

While driving along, the officer had noticed a large, four-door sedan stopped on the right shoulder of the freeway. The officer saw a single adult male sitting in the driver's seat. Thinking that the vehicle might be disabled as a result of a mechanical breakdown, the officer pulled his patrol car over to the shoulder behind the other vehicle and stopped. The officer turned on his warning lights, got out of his patrol car, and walked up to the passenger-side window of the car, which was closed. As the officer came alongside the passenger door, he noticed that the driver was looking straight ahead, seemingly oblivious to the officer's presence.

The officer started tapping on the passenger-side window to get the driver's attention. As he did so, he noticed three men crouched on all fours on the floor of the front seat of the vehicle. One of the men was huddled so close to the driver's legs that he was effectively blocking the driver's feet from touching the gas and brake pedals. "Their heads were so close to the floor that they looked like maybe they were looking for a lost earring or carefully inspecting the floor mat," the officer had recalled.

At first, the driver did not react to the officer's tapping on the window but kept looking straight ahead. Then the officer tapped on the window harder, and the driver turned to look at him. The officer gestured to the driver to open the passenger-side window, and the driver leaned over toward the passenger door and rolled down the window.

The officer pointed at the men crouched on the floor of the vehicle, and asked the driver, "What're they doing there?"

The driver looked straight at the officer with a puzzled expression on his face. Without hesitation, without so much as a glance downward, he spread his hands wide and simply asked, "Who?"

7. “What Did You See When They Opened the Trunk?”

A defendant in denial is like a ship blown badly off course in a storm, making its way without any navigational equipment on a pitiless, raging sea. An inept lawyer is like an aimless iceberg bumbling along just beneath the surface of that indifferent, freezing ocean. When a wayward ship meets an aimless iceberg, God help the poor defendant, for his hull will soon be ripped open, and his ship will sink like a stone. Despite the defendant’s pitiful cries for help and barring a miracle, no angel of salvation will toss him a life preserver in his hour of direst need.

Watching a defendant’s case sink hopelessly is a little bit like witnessing a boat break apart and sink far out on the ocean, while praying that no one is still on board the doomed vessel. For however richly an intractable defendant may deserve his fate, however much he is his own worst enemy, at a minimum, a defendant always deserves a fair trial, and also to be defended if not brilliantly nor successfully, at least competently.

I recall a jury trial of a Spanish-speaking defendant who was accused in a two-count indictment of smuggling cocaine into the United States from Mexico—that is, he knowingly and intentionally imported cocaine into the United States and possessed the same cocaine with the intent to distribute it to others. As the testimony of the government’s witnesses revealed, the defendant faced a serious, circumstantial hurdle in his case. A confidential informant had placed a telephone call ahead of time to an agent of the narcotics task force. The informant had told the agent that he had reliable information that a large load of cocaine was going to be crossed into the United States from Mexico. The informant had described the make and model of the load vehicle to the agent and had told the agent the time and place that the vehicle was supposed to cross the border. Therefore, although the agents did not have prior information about the identity or description of the driver, ultimately it did not matter.

Whoever the driver was, he was "jailbait," because sooner or later, the agents were going to stop and search the car. If they found cocaine in it, the driver was going to be arrested, interrogated, and transported to jail. As their trial testimony revealed, the narcotics task force agents had considered their options and had come up with a plan. They would watch for the suspected load vehicle at the time and place it was supposed to pass through the port of entry. An alert for the vehicle would be placed on the computers in the primary inspection booths, and the inspectors on duty would be watching for the vehicle. Depending on the situation, the inspectors would allow it to pass through the port of entry without sending it to secondary inspection, and hopefully without arousing the driver's suspicion. A small army of unmarked vehicles would then surreptitiously follow the vehicle to its destination. There, also depending on the situation, the agents would attempt to conduct surveillance on the vehicle and its occupant(s).

When the time was right, the agents would stop and search the vehicle and question its occupant(s). By allowing the driver to cross the border and continue on toward his destination unawares, the agents hoped to eventually be able to detain and arrest more of the people suspected to be involved in the cocaine distribution chain. The agents were well aware that things might turn dangerous when they made their move. That is where the small army of unmarked vehicles would come into the picture.

As it turned out, the agents' plan ultimately worked, although not without many more twists and turns than they had foreseen. Sure enough, a car matching the description the informant had given crossed through the port of entry at precisely the time and place the informant had told the agent that it would. A lone male was the driver and sole occupant of the vehicle.

As per the plan, the customs inspector on duty at the primary inspection booth briefly checked the driver's immigration status (the driver did have a valid permit to cross the border) and performed a cursory inspection of the vehicle. The inspector then waved the driver through the port of entry. The vehicle exited the port of entry and headed north through the sprawling border town. As it did so, the small army of unmarked vehicles initiated their pursuit of the suspected load vehicle as discreetly as traffic conditions permitted, but as it turned out, not discreetly enough.

Within seconds, the suspected load vehicle began moving in such a bizarre, erratic manner that the pursuing agents could only conclude that the driver had "made the tail." Without warning, the vehicle would pull over to the side of the road and stop, as though waiting to allow the traffic behind it to pass by. Then, after waiting for a few seconds, it would pull out into traffic again, only to slow down, then speed up, then slow down and pull over once again, then wait for a moment and take off again. When approaching intersections, the vehicle would wait until the last moment, then make an abrupt left or right turn, and repeat a similar process. In the lingo of the narcotics agents, the driver of the vehicle was clearly engaging in "counter surveillance."

The driver's seemingly random route played hell with the pursuing agents' plans. Despite their best efforts, on several occasions the agents had to drive past the suspected load car when it would suddenly pull over to the side of the road. More than once, pursuit team vehicles passed one another driving in the opposite direction. They made a quick decision to back off the pursuit, hoping to make their quarry think that he had "shaken the tail."

Even after the agents had terminated their active pursuit, the suspected load driver continued to drive erratically for another fifteen to twenty minutes. Finally, he turned onto the main road north and drove out of town into the surrounding farm country.

While the soon-to-be defendant drove out into the flat farmland on the outskirts of the town, the small army of narcotics task force agents quickly regrouped. They changed vehicles, then resumed their pursuit of the suspected load car at what they hoped was a considerably more discreet distance. They observed the vehicle make a couple of turns at four-way intersections, and finally saw it turn into the dirt driveway of what appeared to be an abandoned farmhouse. The house was surrounded on all sides by flat fields tilled for cultivation.

Watching through high-powered binoculars, the agents saw the driver park the car in the empty farmyard, then get out and walk straight to the raised front porch. He walked quickly up the steps onto the porch, went straight to the front door, and let himself into the house, apparently using a key and without knocking first.

Given the lack of nearby cover and suitable places from which to set up surveillance of the house and car, the task force agents parked their numerous vehicles much farther away from the property than they would have liked. Their hope, as one of them testified at trial, was that the driver would think that they were vehicles belonging to farm workers who were coming to work in the neighboring fields, and that he would not make a run for it.

So began a mutual game of peek-a-boo that lasted for several hours. Every so often, the surveillance teams would see the front door of the house open, and the driver step out onto the porch. The driver would look around, as though watching for someone or waiting for something to happen. Then he would go back inside the house and close the door. For their part, the agents stayed put.

Hours passed, and of the few other vehicles that passed by the property, not one of them was observed to even slow down, much less turn off the highway and enter the farmyard. To the agents, it looked more and more like the suspected load car driver had been left holding the bag. Whoever he was supposed to meet had not shown up and was not going to show up. The agents surmised that the driver's original plan to rendezvous with his associates and deliver the suspected load vehicle had been scuttled when he realized he was being tailed. At length, the decision was made to move in.

The agents waited until they observed the driver step out onto the porch again. Then they started their vehicles and pulled out onto the highway. As they did so, they observed the driver start to walk fast toward the suspected load vehicle. Just as he was unlocking the driver's side door, the first units of unmarked police vehicles pulled into the driveway, blocking the driver's route of escape. The narcotics task force agents hit the ground running.

Shouting at the driver to put his hands up, the agents quickly approached him with guns drawn and trained on him. One agent pushed him facedown onto the hood of the car, took the car keys away from him, then frisked him and handcuffed him. This agent then escorted the driver a short distance away from the car and remained with him while several armed agents quickly surrounded the house, burst inside and determined that it was empty. Then the team converged on the suspected load vehicle.

One of the agents asked the driver in Spanish for permission to search the car. The driver shrugged and told him to go ahead, that the car wasn't his, and he didn't care. The search didn't take long. Nothing out of the ordinary was found in the passenger compartment. Then one of the agents inserted the key and opened the trunk. He found the entire trunk piled high with tightly wrapped kilo-sized packages. They were stacked in plain view and looked very much like the kind of packages that might contain cocaine.

Taking out a pocketknife, one of the agents cut a small hole in one of the packages and removed a small sample of the white powdery substance that was inside. Using a field test kit, the agent performed a preliminary test on the sample, which tested positive for cocaine. The agent then put the sampled package and test kit inside a plastic bag, sealed it, placed it back in the trunk with the other packages, and closed the trunk.

As soon as the agent finished performing the preliminary field test, the agent who had handcuffed the load car driver and escorted him away from the car placed him under arrest for importation and possession of cocaine with the intent to distribute it. They had the defendant sit in the back seat of one of their cars as they transported him back to the narcotics task force office located next to the port of entry. A pair of agents drove the load vehicle (with the cocaine still in the trunk) back to the office, escorted and protected by the small army of unmarked cars.

Once back at their office, a number of the agents methodically processed the load in order to identify the seizure and to preserve representative samples of the suspected cocaine in the event the case were to go trial. Soon, the entire load, now packaged in sealed boxes each marked with an evidence label, was on its way to the Drug Enforcement Administration (DEA) laboratory. In due course, a laboratory chemist performed a chemical analysis of ten random core samples taken from ten sample packages as well as a sample taken from one representative kilo-sized package. The chemical analysis of the samples enabled the chemist to form a definitive opinion that every one of the analyzed samples contained cocaine hydrochloride.

While the suspected contraband was being processed, the case agent and another agent escorted the defendant inside the building and walked him to an interview room. Once inside, they removed his handcuffs and sat him down at a desk. One of the agents read out loud to the defendant a Spanish-language version of the Miranda rights. They asked him if he understood his rights, and he said that he did. They asked him if he was willing to answer questions without an attorney being present. The defendant replied that he wished to speak to an attorney and did not wish to answer any questions. The interview ended quickly, and very soon the defendant found himself being transported to jail.

Because the drug-smuggling charges filed against the defendant exposed him to a ten-year mandatory minimum prison sentence, and because the defendant was a Mexican citizen and resident with few solid ties to the United States, the federal prosecutors believed that if he were to be released on bail pending trial, it was highly likely that he would flee to Mexico to avoid prosecution. For this reason, the prosecutors made a motion to the court to detain the defendant without bail. The court held a detention hearing and agreed with the prosecutors that the defendant posed a serious flight risk. Therefore, the court granted the government's motion to detain the defendant without bail. As a consequence, the defendant spent several months in the federal jail, waiting for his trial to begin.

While in jail, the defendant did not sit around wringing his hands and bemoaning his fate. For one thing, he decided that his court-appointed attorney was paying far too little attention to his case, so within a short time, he hired a private attorney to defend him. However, by the time the private attorney entered the case, the federal prosecutor had already turned over the agents' investigative reports to the defendant's court-appointed attorney. The attorney had dutifully reviewed the reports with his client. In this way, the defendant learned that there had been a confidential informant in his case who had given a tip to the federal agents. Very belatedly, the defendant came to the bitter realization that he had been hung out to dry—that his cocaine-smuggling run had been doomed to failure from the outset.

Evidently, this realization did not sit well with the defendant. To judge by his self-righteous indignation on the witness stand, the defendant took himself very seriously. He considered himself an intelligent, decisive man of action, not a simpleminded dupe to be trifled with. His testimony at trial clearly reflected that he had thought long and hard about how to turn the tables on those who had made a fool out of him.

Meanwhile, as the time for trial drew near, the defense attorney had hardly been idle either. In court, during pretrial hearings, he seemed haggard and careworn, as though he had perhaps been working long hours on a defense. Still the days dwindled down. At long last, apparently because no defense had as yet materialized, the defense attorney decided to pull out all the stops. He would take his briefcase in hand, walk the few short blocks from his office to the federal jail, and visit his client. He would sit down and talk with his Spanish-speaking client for the first time since his initial visit, when the defendant had signed their retainer agreement. Over the years, it had become painfully clear to the interpreting staff that the defense attorney had the utmost confidence in his ability to understand and speak Spanish. Therefore, he saw no need to hire an interpreter to accompany him to the jail and would visit his client by himself.

The defense attorney was no "Johnny-come-lately" to the courtroom. He liked to think that after spending a number of years representing tricky, cunning criminals, he was a shrewd judge of character. It gave him satisfaction to think that his considerable experience had endowed him with an almost uncanny knack for taking the measure of a man and gauging his truth and veracity. So, he sat with his client in a visiting room and looked him right in the eye.

Speaking in his garbled Spanish, the defense attorney asked the defendant to explain to him exactly how he had come to be driving the load vehicle on the day of his arrest, and why he had driven so strangely after he left the port of entry. The defendant purported to tell his attorney the whole truth and nothing but the truth about the entire sequence of events. As the defense attorney sat and listened, he was gripped by a sudden realization that this man sitting across from him was a very eloquent speaker who had personally witnessed and vividly recalled all of the events that had transpired on the day of his arrest. As the defendant recounted his version of events, his attorney also realized that the defendant was unshakably convinced of his own innocence. For a brief moment, the attorney regretted not having sat down to interview the defendant weeks before in order to initiate an appropriate follow-up investigation. After all, if the defendant's statement were true, such an investigation might well have turned up some helpful character witnesses, or perhaps even some corroborating exculpatory testimony or evidence. As his client finished telling the story of his arrest, the attorney continued to listen intently, nod his head, and take notes. He dismissed his fleeting regret at not having sought any independent verification of the defendant's story. In the end, the attorney looked his client right in the eye and believed every word he said.

Just like that, attorney and client meshed. The two of them put their heads together and hit upon a bold, brilliant strategy. The defense would deliver a shocking, devastating right-to-the-jaw of the prosecution. During the trial, the defense would call no other witnesses besides the defendant. Why should they? The defendant would take the witness stand and testify. He would tell the jury the whole truth and nothing but the truth about the entire chain of events, just as he had told his attorney. It would be a daring, all-or-nothing roll-of-the-dice that just might convince the jury that not only was the defendant innocent, but in fact he had been framed.

So, the first day of trial arrived. The judge to whom the case was assigned was a no-nonsense veteran. Over the years, he had presided with a firm, fair hand over innumerable trials involving the same kinds of charges—drug smuggling or alien smuggling. He was an intelligent, competent, practical judge—a judge who knew how to get to the heart of the matter and not complicate things for no good reason.

By noon on the first day, the jury had been selected, and the judge had given his preliminary instructions to the jury. Once the trial resumed after the noonday recess, both lawyers made their opening statements to the jury.

The prosecutor briefly outlined for the jury what he expected the prosecution's evidence would show. He named the witnesses that he expected to call and summarized the facts to which he expected each of the witnesses would testify. He touched on the elements of the two charges in the indictment and noted that it was his burden to prove each of the elements of both charges beyond a reasonable doubt. He also mentioned that among the elements that the government had to prove, the one and only element in real dispute was the defendant's knowledge. In other words, for the jury to find the defendant guilty of importing cocaine, they would have to find beyond a reasonable doubt that the defendant had known that he was importing cocaine or some other prohibited drug into the United States. For the jury to find the defendant guilty of possessing cocaine with the intent to distribute it, they would have to find that the defendant knew that there was cocaine or some other prohibited drug in the car that he had driven across the border on the day of the offense.

The prosecutor thanked the jury for their attention. He concluded by expressing his confidence that after the jury had listened to all of the evidence, the closing arguments of counsel and the court's instructions, and after they had carefully considered the facts of the case, that they would be convinced beyond a reasonable doubt that the defendant had been proven guilty of both charges, and that they would return a verdict of guilty on both counts.

Then it was the defense attorney's turn to make his opening statement to the jury. He thanked the members of the jury for their willingness to serve. He told them that he sincerely empathized with the profound duty they had all sworn to fulfill. He assured them that he understood that it is never an easy thing to pass judgment on another human being. In fact, he told them, one of the most important things they would have to judge in the case for which they had been selected was the credibility of the witnesses who would be testifying.

He told the jurors that they would have a very difficult decision to make, because they would soon be hearing two diametrically opposite, mutually irreconcilable versions of some of the events that had occurred on the day his client was arrested.

"In case anyone on the jury does not know the meaning of the term 'diametrically opposite,'" he said, "it's just one of those fancy terms that lawyers like to use, and it means 'directly contrary or opposite to.'" As he explained, the jury would see that both versions of events could not be true, so their decision as to whose testimony they believed would be crucial to their verdict in the case.

He reminded the jury that they had already heard from the court that a defendant in a criminal case has no burden to testify in his own defense, that the defendant does not have to do one single thing to prove his innocence. He then told the jury, "I'm going to let you all in on a little secret right now, and that is that Mr. Blanco *is* going to testify in his own defense. Why? Because, as you will soon see, in this case Mr. Blanco is not merely *not guilty* beyond a reasonable doubt. In fact, he is absolutely innocent of these charges, and he has nothing to fear. So he will be taking the stand to tell you exactly what he did and what he saw—" and here the defense attorney paused and stared intensely at the jury—"and exactly what he did *not* do and did *not* see on the day of his arrest."

The defense attorney paused again for dramatic effect, as if to let his last remark ricochet around inside the skull cavities of the jurors for a while. He stood with his hands gripping the sides of the podium, staring off into the distance as though pondering the imponderable. At length, he forged onward: "Ladies and gentlemen, I am the first to admit that what you will soon hear from the mouth of Mr. Blanco will sound strange, perhaps even incredible. Nevertheless, in this case, the defendant will prove to you beyond a reasonable doubt that he could not possibly have known that there was cocaine in the car that he was driving. Members of the jury, it is almost as though Mr. Blanco is the prosecutor in reverse. He will prove to you beyond a reasonable doubt that he is innocent. Now I can just see those wheels turning around inside your minds. I'd be willing to bet that you may be asking yourselves, 'How will he prove it to me?' Well, at the risk of keeping you in suspense for a little while longer, I will let Mr. Blanco speak for himself. Now Mr. Blanco has been waiting anxiously for months to tell his story, so when he takes the stand, I just ask you to pay very close attention to his demeanor as well as his words. At the end of this case, ladies and gentlemen, I am confident that you will not just have some flimsy, vague sense of doubt that Mr. Blanco is guilty. Instead, I am confident that you will know deep down in your hearts that he is one hundred and ten percent innocent, and you will return the only just and true verdict in this case—a verdict of not guilty. Thank you, members of the jury." With that, the defense attorney sat down.

Thereafter, the federal prosecutor presented his case-in-chief. In reasonably short order, he called a series of witnesses to prove the two charges against the defendant. The first witness was the narcotics task force agent who had received the tip from the informant. He was followed by the immigration inspector from the primary inspection booth at the port of entry. The prosecutor then called to the stand a small number of the large group of narcotics task force agents who had taken part in the pursuit of the load vehicle as well as the surveillance of the defendant at the farmhouse.

The thankless task of reconstructing the driver's roundabout route of travel fell mainly to one of the agents who had tried to coordinate the efforts of the pursuit team. With the court's permission, the prosecutor had the witness step down from the witness stand. The prosecutor asked the witness to illustrate his testimony using a large map of the city streets where the pursuit had occurred. The witness stood next to the map, which had been placed on an easel in front of the jury box. Using a pointer and some felt marker pens, he tried gamely to accurately describe and diagram for the jury the route taken by the load vehicle. Not unexpectedly, given the nature of the task, the witness's description never made it to the finish line. Within minutes, the map was covered with so many cramped abbreviations, overlapping arrows, and crisscrossing lines that it looked like a hopelessly tangled ball of kite string.

As one of the interpreters assigned to the trial, I had a good view of the jury from where I was sitting. While the witness dutifully continued to describe and diagram the defendant's lurching turns from one street onto the next, one could see the keen attentiveness on the faces of the jurors gradually sag into a glazed look of stupefaction. By now, the diagram was looking more and more like a valiant effort to chart the flight of a drunken bumble bee. Nevertheless, the prosecutor pressed on, prompting his witness to indicate on the map where the defendant had driven next.

The witness also soldiered on, making still more lines and arrows on the map, until finally he paused. He stood next to the map, looking sheepishly at the tangled mess he had laboriously drawn at the prosecutor's request. Finally, he shook his head, looked at the prosecutor apologetically, shrugged his shoulders and confessed to the jury, "I'm sorry. I can't recall exactly where the driver went after that. I do know that he continued to drive around and around for a while until he finally returned to the main highway out of town."

When the witness said this, a number of relieved grins broke out on the faces of some of the jurors. They shifted in their chairs and stretched, as though to rouse themselves from a dream. "Thank you, Agent Ramirez," said the prosecutor. "You may return to the witness stand."

In spite of the witness's incomplete description, his testimony established conclusively that as soon as the defendant had driven the load vehicle out of the port of entry, he had begun driving in a bizarre manner, and had continued to do so for quite a long time. Why might a person drive so nonsensically? Perhaps he was completely insane. Perhaps he was single-mindedly seeking an address that did not exist. Still, when the time came to weigh such testimony, a sensible jury would be hard-pressed not to draw the reasonable conclusion that the defendant had driven erratically because he was trying to elude his pursuers, and that he had continued to drive erratically until he was sure that he had thrown them off his trail. Alas, the defendant had been badly mistaken.

The prosecutor went on to call to the witness stand the agent who had handcuffed and arrested the defendant, followed by a series of agents who had searched the load vehicle, discovered the cocaine in the trunk, seized and processed the suspected narcotics, and submitted the drug samples to the DEA laboratory for chemical analysis. Through the testimony of one of the agents who had participated in the processing of the seized contraband, the prosecutor introduced and offered into evidence a heat-sealed plastic bag which contained a representative sample of cocaine along with one kilo-sized package of cocaine. The heat-sealed bag was marked with a label recording the date of the seizure and the seizure identification number that had been assigned to the evidence. In this way, the prosecutor sought to prove to the jury that the sample and kilo of cocaine admitted into evidence in the courtroom were part of the load seized from the vehicle that the defendant had been driving on the day of his arrest.

The prosecutor then called the DEA laboratory chemist who had performed the chemical analyses of the samples and had formed the expert opinion that all of the samples contained cocaine hydrochloride. Finally, the prosecutor called to the witness stand a very experienced special agent from the United States Customs Service. After a brief hearing, the judge made the requisite finding that the agent was sufficiently experienced and knowledgeable to testify as an expert witness regarding distributable amounts of cocaine and the current wholesale price per kilogram of cocaine on the street. The agent then testified that in his expert opinion, the substantial amount of cocaine imported by the defendant was intended for distribution, and further, that during the period of time when the defendant had been arrested, the amount of cocaine seized from the vehicle driven by the defendant had a wholesale value in the United States well in excess of half a million dollars.

The defense attorney had few if any questions for most of the prosecution's witnesses. He cross-examined each of the witnesses who had taken part in the pursuit of the suspected load vehicle, seeking to establish whether all of the pursuit vehicles were unmarked cars, and if all of the agents had been dressed in plain clothes. Each of the witnesses answered that all of the pursuit vehicles were unmarked cars, and that so far as they could recall, all of the agents involved in the pursuit had been dressed in plain clothes.

He then asked the witnesses if, as far as they knew, there had been anything at all about their vehicles, their clothing, the way they had pursued the suspected load vehicle, or anything else that may have given the defendant reason to believe that he was being followed by law enforcement. Each of the witnesses answered that they had done their best not to "tip off" the defendant in any way that they were law enforcement agents, and that they were following him.

When it came time for the defense attorney to cross-examine the agent who had handcuffed the defendant and then escorted him a short distance away from the load vehicle, the defense attorney asked the agent how far away from the car he had walked the defendant, and if he had escorted the defendant to a point from where the defendant would have been able to watch the agents searching the car. He particularly wanted to know if the defendant would have been able to see the area of the trunk of the car.

In response, the witness estimated that he had escorted the handcuffed defendant approximately thirty to forty feet away from the load vehicle. He acknowledged that it was quite possible that the defendant might have been able to watch and see at least part of the search of the vehicle from that vantage point. The witness could not recall if the defendant would have been able to see the area of the trunk of the car from the spot where the two of them had been standing.

By the beginning of the afternoon session of the second day of trial, the prosecutor had finished the presentation of his case-in-chief, reconfirmed that he had duly moved all his exhibits into evidence, and had rested. The court then addressed the defense attorney and asked him if he wished to present any evidence or call any witnesses.

"Yes, Your Honor," the defense attorney replied. "The defense calls the defendant, Mr. Blanco, to the stand."

Much as he had done on that momentous day when he visited his client in the federal jail, the defense attorney asked the defendant to explain to the jury exactly how he had come to be driving the load vehicle on the day of his arrest. Through the question-and-answer process of his direct examination, the defendant gave the following explanation.

The defendant lived in Mexicali. By his own description, he was a self-employed mechanic and handyman who needed work. Late on the morning of the day on which the defendant was arrested, he had met a man at a bar in Mexicali. He and the man had introduced themselves and had told one another their first names. The defendant did not know the full name of his new acquaintance, nor his telephone number, address, or how to locate him. The two of them had struck up a conversation over a couple of beers, and the man had asked him if he was interested in making some money. The defendant had asked the man how, and the man had told him that he had a house out in the countryside on the other side of the border. The man needed someone to do some repair work and painting on the house to get it ready to rent.

According to the defendant, the man had told him that he had some errands to run, so he could not go to the house right then, but he would arrive a couple of hours later. The defendant had told the man that he was interested in doing the work, but that his own car was not working. The man had then offered to let the defendant take his car. According to the defendant, the man had seemed nice and trustworthy, so he agreed to go and have a look at the job.

The man had explained to him how to get to the house. He had given the defendant the keys to the car and also to the house, so that the defendant could go inside and assess the work. So, he and the other man parted company, and the defendant drove straight to the port of entry.

The defense attorney then asked the defendant to explain to the jury why he had driven in such an erratic manner after leaving the port of entry. The defendant explained that as soon as he had passed through the port of entry, he had seen a couple of cars that looked like they were following him. He had no idea why anyone would want to follow him, and he got very scared. He had heard about people being kidnapped for ransom on the Mexican side of the border. He had surmised that the people following him might be kidnappers or thugs, that maybe they had mistaken him for someone else. He was terrified and drove so erratically because he wanted to get away from them, whoever they were. Finally, he thought that he had eluded his pursuers, and drove out of town to the farmhouse.

Once he arrived at the farmhouse, he explained that he had gone inside and assessed the work that needed to be done. Then he just waited around for his prospective employer to show up. Hours passed, and he was getting impatient. Finally, he had given up hope that the man would arrive and decided to return to Mexicali to look for him. He was just getting back into the car to head back to Mexicali when a large number of narcotics agents appeared out of the blue, shouting at him, pointing their pistols at him, pushing him down on the hood of the car, frisking him, handcuffing him, and ultimately arresting him.

"Now, Mr. Blanco," said the defense attorney, "I want you to carefully explain to the jury exactly what happened after the agent handcuffed you and escorted you away from the car that you had driven earlier that day."

"First of all," replied the defendant, "it is not true that he escorted me to a distance of thirty or forty feet away from the car. In fact, he just pulled me two or three steps away from the car."

The defense attorney then asked the defendant to describe to the jury what he saw next.

"I saw two or three agents climbing into the car, looking around inside it, and feeling underneath the seats with their hands. Then I saw one of the agents put the key into the trunk lock and open the trunk of the car."

"Now, Mr. Blanco, when you saw the agent open the trunk, were you close enough to be able to see clearly inside the trunk?"

"Yes, I was just a few feet away, and I could see the whole interior of the trunk."

"Mr. Blanco—" began the defense attorney, and he paused. He stood with his hands gripping the sides of the podium, staring intensely at the defendant, who stared right back at him. "—I want you to look directly at the jury and answer this question: What did you see when they opened the trunk?"

The defendant slowly turned and looked solemnly at the jury. "Nothing!" he pronounced dramatically.

"You saw *nothing*?" asked the defense attorney.

"I saw nothing!" replied the defendant.

"Mr. Blanco," asked the defense attorney, "when you say you saw nothing inside the trunk, are you saying that you did not see the packages of cocaine that the agents have testified that they found inside the trunk of the vehicle that you had driven earlier that day?"

"How could I see those packages if they weren't there?" replied the defendant.

"Mr. Blanco," said the defense attorney, "let me be absolutely sure that I understand your testimony to this jury. Are you testifying that you just did not see the packages of what later turned out to be cocaine in the trunk, or are you testifying that the packages were not there?"

"As I said before, I could see the whole interior of the trunk of the car. I could clearly see that there were no packages in the trunk. The trunk was empty. There was no cocaine."

"Now, Mr. Blanco," continued the defense attorney, "I want you to look directly at the jury and answer this question: Did you know that there was cocaine in the car that you had driven earlier that day?"

The defendant again turned slowly to face the jury and smiled triumphantly. "How could I know there was cocaine in the car if there was no cocaine in the car?" he replied.

"Mr. Blanco," asked the defense attorney, "How can you be so sure that there was no cocaine in the trunk of the car?"

"I can say with absolute certainty that there was no cocaine in the car," replied the defendant, "because I looked in the trunk before I drove the car to the border just to make sure that I would not have any problems when I came to the inspection at the port of entry, and the trunk was empty. Then, as I have already told you, when the agent opened the trunk with the key, I could see inside the trunk, and it was still empty."

The defense attorney then asked, "Mr. Blanco, please explain to the jury what made you look in the trunk of the car before you drove it to the border. I mean what kinds of problems did you think you might have at the port of entry?"

"I looked in the trunk because I have heard stories from other people that sometimes drug smugglers hide drugs in cars, and they ask people to drive the cars through the port of entry without telling the drivers that there are drugs in the car," answered the defendant.

The defense attorney then looked at the defendant, and asked, "Mr. Blanco, earlier today, while you were sitting in this courtroom, did you hear the agent testify about how he discovered the packages of cocaine in the trunk of the car that you had driven, and did you see the samples of cocaine that he testified came from the packages in the trunk of the car?"

"Yes, I heard him testify that he found the drugs in the trunk of the car, and I saw the samples of the drugs that he says came from the packages in the trunk. He is lying, because I saw with my own eyes that there was no cocaine in the trunk of the car," replied the defendant.

"Thank you, Mr. Blanco," said the defense attorney. "No further questions, Your Honor."

I happened to be interpreting for the defendant as he unequivocally testified that there had been no packages of cocaine piled high in the trunk of the car, and that the agent who had so testified was lying. From my vantage point next to the witness stand, I glimpsed a very slight change in the expressions on the faces of the prosecutor and the case agent sitting next to him at the counsel table. The two of them relaxed ever so slightly in their chairs. I also glanced over at the jury. More than one of them had smiles on their faces. At the same time, the whole feeling in the courtroom abruptly changed. All of a sudden, whatever drama had gripped the proceedings until that moment was gone. It was a funny feeling, almost like the air had been let out of a tire.

It was now the prosecutor's turn to cross-examine the defendant. The prosecutor stood at the podium and smiled at the defendant. "Good afternoon, Mr. Blanco," he said.

"Good afternoon," the defendant replied.

"Mr. Blanco," said the prosecutor, "I just have a few questions for you. Do you know why you were arrested in this case?"

"Because the agents say that they found cocaine in the car that I was driving, but that is not true," answered the defendant.

"Mr. Blanco, were you sitting here in the courtroom, and did you hear Agent Vasquez testify about how he arrested you?" asked the prosecutor.

"Yes," responded the defendant.

"Did you hear Agent Vasquez testify under oath before this jury that when he arrested you, he told you that you were under arrest for importation of cocaine and for possession of cocaine with the intent to distribute it?" asked the prosecutor.

"He just told me that I was under arrest because I had cocaine in the car that I had driven across the border, but that was a lie," replied the defendant.

"So, Agent Vasquez did tell you that you were under arrest because there was cocaine in the car that you had driven across the border, is that right?" asked the prosecutor.

"Yes, but as I already told you, that is a lie, because there was no cocaine," responded the defendant.

"Mr. Blanco, is it your testimony to this jury that the agents arrested you for importation of cocaine and possession of cocaine, and that they took you to jail even though they found no cocaine in the car that you had been driving earlier that day?" asked the prosecutor.

"Yes, that is my testimony," replied the defendant.

"Mr. Blanco, were you sitting here in the courtroom, and did you see the samples of cocaine that Agent Walters says that he discovered and later removed from the trunk of the car that you had driven earlier that day—the same samples which have now been admitted into evidence in this trial?" asked the prosecutor.

"Yes, I saw them, but they were not in the trunk of the car when the agent opened the trunk. As I have already said, I could see clearly into the interior of the trunk, and it was empty," replied the defendant.

"Mr. Blanco, why did the agents arrest you if there was no cocaine in the car that you had driven?" asked the prosecutor.

"I don't know why. Why don't you ask him?" replied the defendant, pointing as he spoke at the case agent who was sitting at the counsel table, and looking back at him intently.

"Mr. Blanco, are you insinuating that the agents in this case arrested you even though there was no cocaine in the car that you had been driving, then took you back to the narcotics task force office, and then put the cocaine in the trunk of the car back at their office?" asked the prosecutor.

"I can't say for sure. All I know is that they are the ones who had the car in their custody after they arrested me, and that there was no cocaine in the car when I was arrested. Why don't you ask him?" replied the defendant, pointing once again at the case agent. Then he plunged ahead: "He is the one who has connections with informants. What is more, there are rumors that Agent Juarez has connections to some of the biggest drug trafficking organizations in the Mexicali area."

As the defendant testified, I looked at the case agent. He was staring studiously at his notepad and laboring hard to jot something down, but his face had turned a shade redder, and a grimace or perhaps a struggle not to smile was tugging persistently at the corners of his mouth.

"Mr. Blanco," continued the prosecutor, "you testified that after you drove out of the port of entry, you thought you saw cars following you, and that you got scared because you thought they were maybe kidnappers or bad people, and that you thought maybe they were following you by mistake; is that right?"

"That's right," responded the defendant.

"And you drove around and around the city streets for fifteen or twenty minutes, until you felt certain that you were no longer being followed by the kidnappers or bad people; is that right?" asked the prosecutor.

"Yes," answered the defendant.

"Mr. Blanco, did you ever drive to the police station to ask for help or try to signal a passing police car to ask for help?" asked the prosecutor.

"No," said the defendant.

"Why not? If you knew that there were no drugs in the car that you were driving, and if you had nothing to fear, why did you not just drive straight to the police station to seek protection?" asked the prosecutor.

"I got very scared and lost my head," replied the defendant. "I didn't know who the people were or why they might be following me, but I got very scared and didn't know what to do," replied the defendant.

"Mr. Blanco, as a self-employed handyman, did you have any of your tools with you in the car that you drove through the port of entry—tools such as a tape measure, for example?" asked the prosecutor.

"No, my tools were in my car, which was not working at the time. Besides, as I have already testified, I was just going to take a look at the work that needed to be done at the house, and give the man an estimate," answered the defendant.

"Just one final question, Mr. Blanco," said the prosecutor. "If you had never been there before, how did you know how to get to that farmhouse in particular? Did the man who you were supposed to meet there give you written directions?"

"No, he did not give me written directions. He just explained to me how to get there, and I have a good memory," answered the defendant.

"Thank you, Mr. Blanco. No further questions, Your Honor," said the prosecutor.

Because the defendant was the only witness called by the defense, the prosecutor then had his opportunity to present his rebuttal case. He called two rebuttal witnesses. First, he recalled to the witness stand Agent Walters, who had opened the trunk and discovered the cocaine inside. The prosecutor showed the agent the cocaine samples that had been admitted into evidence earlier. He asked the agent if he still recognized the samples, and where he had first seen them. To nobody's surprise, the agent answered that he still recognized the samples of cocaine, and that he had first seen them when he had opened the trunk of the car parked in the farmyard on the afternoon of the defendant's arrest. The prosecutor then asked Agent Walters if it was possible that he was mistaken, and if the trunk of the car had in fact been empty when he opened it. The agent looked puzzled, and replied, "Excuse me, I don't understand the question." The prosecutor repeated the question. The agent smiled, shook his head, and replied, "No, sir. I am not mistaken. The trunk of the car was not empty." The prosecutor then asked the agent if he was absolutely certain that there had been cocaine in the trunk of the car when he opened it. The agent smiled again and replied that he was absolutely certain.

The prosecutor then called to the witness stand Agent Vasquez, who had arrested the defendant. He asked the agent on what charges the defendant had been arrested, to which the agent replied that the defendant had been arrested on charges of importation of cocaine and possession of cocaine with the intent to distribute it. The prosecutor then asked the agent if upon his return to the narcotics task force office after the arrest of the defendant, he had placed the cocaine in the trunk of the car that the defendant had driven earlier that day. The agent shook his head, and said, "No, sir." The prosecutor then asked the agent if he had seen any of his fellow officers on the narcotics task force place cocaine in the trunk of the car on the day of the defendant's arrest. The agent again shook his head, and replied, "No, sir." The prosecutor then asked the agent if narcotics task force officers would have arrested the defendant that day if there had been no cocaine in the trunk of the car that he had driven. The agent again shook his head, and replied, "No, sir." Finally, the prosecutor asked the agent if the narcotics task force wants to arrest an innocent person, do they keep a multiple-kilogram supply of cocaine handy in case an opportunity arises to stash it in the person's car without the person knowing. The agent smiled broadly, and started to shake his head no, when the defense attorney leapt to his feet and objected. Even before the court could rule on the objection, the prosecutor said, "I'll withdraw the question, Your Honor. I have no further questions for the witness." The defense attorney had no questions for either of the prosecutor's rebuttal witnesses, and so both sides rested.

The rest of the trial, which included the lawyers' closing arguments and the instructions of the court, turned out to be anticlimactic. The prosecutor methodically reviewed the evidence presented and the elements of the two charges against the defendant. He noted that the defense has no burden to present any evidence at all to prove the defendant's innocence, but that if the defense elects to present evidence, the jury should judge the evidence presented by the defense in the same way that it judges all the other evidence in the case. He left it up to the jury to decide if the narcotics task force agents had hatched a scheme to frame an innocent man. In closing, he argued that both charges against the defendant had been proven beyond a reasonable doubt. He asked the jury to consider the evidence in the case fully and fairly, apply the law to the facts, and return a verdict of guilty on both counts.

The defense attorney then addressed the jury. He sought to frame the case as a classic contest of witness credibility, and asked the jury to ask themselves if the prosecutor had disproved the defendant's claim that there had been no cocaine in the trunk of the car that he had driven on the day of his arrest. He played down the inference of guilty knowledge that could be drawn from the defendant's erratic pattern of driving the load vehicle once he exited the port of entry. After all, he reminded the jury, the agents had all testified that they had done everything within their power to not "tip off" the defendant that he was being followed by law enforcement. He asked the jury, "Why shouldn't the defendant have thought that he was being followed by kidnappers or thugs?"

He then called the jury's attention to one of the instructions that the court would soon be giving them. The instruction was to the effect that if the evidence was susceptible to two reasonable interpretations—one pointing to the defendant's innocence and the other pointing to the defendant's guilt—then the jury should of course adopt the interpretation pointing to the defendant's innocence. The defense attorney did not come right out and ask the jury to determine if the prosecution's witnesses had committed perjury on the witness stand, or if they had conspired to frame an innocent man. Instead he stood at the podium and paused for what he deemed an appropriately dramatic moment. Once again, he stared intensely at the jury and said, "Ladies and gentlemen of the jury, sometimes truth *is* stranger than fiction." Then he asked the jury to stop and ask themselves a question: why in the world would a defendant accused of such a serious crime make up such an improbable claim unless it was true, much less attest to its truth under penalty of perjury before a judge and jury?"

The defense attorney never explicitly argued that if the defendant were going to make up a whopper, he certainly could have made up a better whopper than the one he had told the jury. Nevertheless, as I interpreted the remainder of the defense attorney's closing remarks, it gradually dawned on me that he was essentially asking the jury to find the defendant not guilty simply because his story was so farfetched that it had to be true. The defense attorney reminded the jury that he had told them in his opening statement that he was confident that by the end of the trial, they would know in their hearts that the defendant was innocent, because he could not have known that there was cocaine in the car he had driven on the day of his arrest. At the close of his argument, he stared at the jury intensely for one last time and asked them to search their hearts. He asked them to ask themselves if down deep inside, they didn't have at least a pinch or a twinge or even a pang of a reasonable doubt that the defendant was guilty. Once they realized that they did have a pang of doubt, he was convinced that they would feel an enormous weight lifted off their shoulders, because they would then be free to vote their conscience. When they voted their conscience, the defense attorney concluded, they would vote to acquit the defendant of both charges, because they would know not merely that he was not guilty, but that in fact he was one hundred and ten percent innocent. With that, the defense attorney thanked the jury and sat down.

The prosecutor's second and final closing argument was very brief. The court then read its instructions on the law to the jury. By then it was getting late in the afternoon. The court thanked the alternate jurors and excused them from further service in the trial. The court reminded the jurors not to discuss the case, to return to court the following morning at 9:00 to commence their deliberations, and then excused them. Prior to adjourning for the evening, the court instructed the parties, marshals, and court staff to be on call for questions or a verdict as of 9:00 the following morning.

Thus, the defendant had to wait overnight to learn his fate, but when the next morning came, that wait turned out to be very short. As one of the interpreters who had been assigned to the trial, I happened to be on call for the jury deliberations. Shortly before 9:30 a.m., the telephone rang in our office. It was the courtroom deputy calling to say that the jury had a verdict. They had been deliberating for under half an hour following a trial that had lasted two full days.

Within a few minutes, the parties had reassembled in the courtroom, and the jury foreman handed the verdict form to the courtroom deputy. The courtroom deputy handed the verdict form to the judge, who looked it over briefly, handed it back to the courtroom deputy, and asked her to read the verdict. The courtroom deputy stood and read the jury's unanimous verdict of guilty as to both counts against the defendant. The court then asked if either of the parties wished to have the jury polled as to their verdicts, and the defense attorney responded that he did want to have the jury polled. So, the courtroom deputy asked the members of the jury one-by-one if the verdict that had been presented and read was in fact their individual verdict. One-by-one, the members of the jury replied, "Yes." Wayward ship had run smack into aimless iceberg. The knockout punch to the prosecution had missed the target entirely.

I was interpreting for the defendant while the verdict was being published and the jury was being polled. To judge by his reaction, the defendant was deeply dismayed at the jury's decision. He looked down at the table, shaking his head in disbelief. He looked up at the ceiling, then over at the jury, then down at the table again. He muttered under his breath, as the court thanked the jury for their attentiveness and their diligent service and excused them from further service in the trial.

As soon as the jury departed from the courtroom, the court set the date for the defendant's sentencing hearing, and the marshals approached the defendant to take him away. Before the marshals could remove the defendant from the courtroom, however, the defense attorney asked the court if he could have a moment to speak with his client in the courtroom. The court granted his request. For the first and only time throughout the entire trial, the defense attorney asked me if I would interpret for him and his client.

The defense attorney told the defendant that he was sorry things hadn't quite worked out as well as they had hoped. He clapped the defendant on the back and told him to buck up—that although they had unfortunately lost a battle, they had by no means lost the war. First, there was the defendant's sentencing to prepare for, and after that would come the long, drawn-out process of the appeal. The attorney also told him that he felt confident that he had some good ideas up his sleeve for the appeal, and it was still way too early to "give up the ship."

The defendant stared at his attorney with an expression that conveyed utter contempt. Then he launched into a loud, angry diatribe to the effect that he was innocent, that the evidence against him was planted, the agents were liars, and the trial was a farce and a mockery of justice. He questioned why he had paid all that money to his lawyer if he was not going to do anything to defend him. I interpreted into English as much as I could of what the defendant was saying. I interpreted as quietly as I could, but because the defendant was speaking quite loudly, I had to speak loud enough to be sure that the defense attorney could hear me.

As it happened, although court had adjourned, the judge was still sitting on the bench while the defense attorney was conferring with his disgruntled client. When the marshals decided that the attorney-client consultation had gone on long enough and approached the defendant to remove him from the courtroom, the defense attorney looked deeply relieved. As quickly as he could, he gathered up his things and beat a hasty retreat from the courtroom.

The courtroom was now empty, except for the judge, his courtroom deputy, and me. I looked up at the judge and smiled a greeting as I was putting away the interpreting equipment. The judge smiled back and said, "Our friend wasn't too happy with the verdict, was he?"

I shook my head no as I crossed the well with headsets and rolled-up extension cables in my hands. "Damn fool," I said. "That jury was back in nothing flat."

"He'd have been a lot better off if he hadn't lied," said the judge.

Long afterward, I crossed paths with the prosecutor in the courthouse. I remember that I asked him how much time the defendant had received at sentencing. The prosecutor thought for a minute, and said, "Oh yeah, Mr. Blanco—that's the guy that testified that the agents must have put the dope in the trunk of the car. You know, I thought at the time that we had a fairly strong case against the defendant, but whenever you go to trial, there is always an element of uncertainty because you just don't know what a jury will do. But the minute the defendant claimed that the trunk of the car was empty, I knew he was going down."

I do not recall the exact number of months that the prosecutor mentioned, but it amounted to considerably more than ten years in federal prison. He mentioned that the defendant had also received a sentencing enhancement based on so-called "obstruction of justice" (that is, for having perjured himself during his trial testimony), an enhancement that effectively added another year or two to his sentence. Out of curiosity, I asked the prosecutor how much less time he thought the defendant might have gotten if he had opted to plead guilty with a negotiated plea agreement rather than going to trial.

"Only the judge could answer that for sure," he replied, "but I think it's safe to say that Mr. Blanco could have gotten substantially less than half the time he got. His lawyer didn't help him all that much."

"Less than half the time!" I exclaimed. "My God! How in the world could his lawyer have put him on the stand to make a bald-faced claim like that?"

The prosecutor shook his head and smiled. "I don't know," he said. "With defense counsel like that, who needs a prosecutor? I'm just glad that I didn't pay his fees. I'll see you around." With that, he turned and headed down the hallway to court.

8. The Smuggler Who Sang at His Sentencing

Of the tens of thousands of routine criminal cases processed through the courts over the years and duly rendered into so many units of finished justice, there are a few unusual cases that stand out in my memory. Who could forget, for example, the case of the wild geese fillets? It's not every day that you see U.S. Fish and Wildlife Service officers go undercover to "sting" a shady proprietor of a small grocery store with a hand-to-hand sale of wild geese fillets, and then cite him to appear in federal court.

What about the undocumented immigrant who pled guilty to having entered the United States illegally, and then told the judge in mitigation, "Your Honor, I just jumped over to this side of the fence to take a piss"? Then there was the seemingly routine, illegal-entry case of that undocumented alien who suddenly proclaimed to the judge that notwithstanding his outwardly human appearance, he was in fact an extraterrestrial ambassador from Saturn. Who could forget such a close encounter with a bona fide "alien," and the seemingly inexplicable manner of his entry without inspection into the United States from the far reaches of the galaxy? In view of the distinguished Saturnian ambassador's exalted station, and pursuant to the requirements of intergalactic, diplomatic protocol as well as the pertinent provisions of the interplanetary code of criminal procedure, he demanded that his case be transferred to the only earthly body whose universal jurisdiction and legal authority he acknowledged, namely, the all-powerful tribunal of twenty-four wise counselors in Washington, DC!

How many more of these out-of-the-ordinary cases have passed through the courts over the years unnoticed and have long since been forgotten? Who can say? I do recall the case of a repentant defendant who sang at his sentencing, and in so doing brought a considerable measure of comic relief to the solemn environs of the courtroom.

As it happened, to my great good fortune, the defendant spoke and sang in English, so I was not required to interpret his speech nor--thank God--attempt to sing some ghastly, off-the-cuff translation of his country-western lyrics. I just happened to be the interpreter assigned to cover the criminal calendar in that courtroom that day. That was how I happened to hear him belt out the first lines of a jailhouse ditty—a song of repentance and redemption that he had composed while passing the time in jail.

To judge by his accent, the singing defendant was a Texan. He was a blond-haired man who looked to be somewhere in his early-to-mid forties. By all accounts, the defendant was a drifter and a drinker, out of work, and down on his luck. On this particular day, he was appearing before the court to be sentenced on a charge of alien smuggling. Because the defendant was in custody, when his case was called the marshals retrieved him from the holding cells adjacent to the courtroom, escorted him into the courtroom, and had him stand next to his attorney at the podium.

Over the years, the defendant had racked up a string of petty offenses and convictions, including more than one prior conviction for the offense of smuggling aliens. Somewhere along the way, he had learned that you can make a quick buck if you can sneak a load of undocumented aliens over the border between Mexico and the United States and deliver them safely to a drop house without being caught by the Border Patrol. Unfortunately for the defendant, on several prior occasions, he had been caught at the border and prosecuted, so his chances of successfully smuggling aliens, drugs, or anything else over the border were slim to none. Still he kept at it, and to no one's surprise, he just kept getting caught. To his credit, whenever he got caught, and he knew perfectly well that he was guilty as charged, he had the grace and good sense to plead guilty and not drag things out unnecessarily.

On the day of his sentencing, the judge made his preliminary remarks and findings for the record, after which the two attorneys gave their sentencing recommendations. In keeping with the negotiated plea agreement, and based on the federal sentencing guidelines, both attorneys recommended that the defendant serve two years, nine months in federal prison. The judge then asked the defendant if he wished to say anything prior to the imposition of sentence.

The defendant stated that he would like to say how truly remorseful he was for having violated the law again. He apologized to the court and stated that he knew he had done wrong by trying to smuggle people across the border again. He wanted the court to know that he knew he had also done wrong things in the past, but that he was not a bad or violent person, and that he did not mean to harm anyone when he drove the car with the people hidden in a dangerous manner inside the vehicle. He wanted the court to know that this time he had learned his lesson once and for all. He assured the court that he foresaw no more smuggling of aliens in his future. Most of all, he wanted the court to know that during the time he had spent in custody, he had been reading the Bible and finding direction and redemption in the Holy Scripture. He knew well that he was a poor sinner, but while in jail, he had come to ask Jesus to forgive him of his sins. To his joyous amazement, Jesus forgave him, and he accepted Jesus Christ as his savior. As a result of having repented his sins and asked the Lord's forgiveness, he felt like a new man. He had always liked to sing and compose country-western songs on the guitar, and while sitting in jail, he had composed a song to express his newfound faith and redemption in the eyes of the Lord. He then said to the court in his fine Texas drawl, "In fact, I'll sing it to you right now, if you like, Your Honor."

A small, sly, wonderful smile lit the judge's face. "Well, I don't know," he said. "I've never had anyone sing before. Does the prosecutor have any objection?"

The prosecutor shook his head no, and said, "No, Your Honor. I have no objection if the defendant wishes to sing his song."

The judge then asked the defense attorney if he objected to the defendant singing his song, to which the defense attorney replied no.

The judge then told the defendant, "All right, go ahead then and sing if you want to."

"I don't have a guitar, so I'll just sing it the best I can," said the defendant. "The first verse goes like this," he said, and he sang:

"I was sittin' in the county ja-il,
thinkin' how my life is he-ll
without the Lord in my life
for so many years… "

The defendant finished singing the first verse and then sang the chorus. With his pronounced drawl, the defendant made "hell" rhyme with "jail," which was a bit of a stretch. All in all, though, he had a pretty fair singing voice, and the part of his song that he sang bespoke his fall from grace, his joyful acceptance of Jesus Christ as his savior, and his gratitude for his newfound redemption in the presence of the Lord. As he sang, various spectators around the courtroom exchanged appreciative glances and nods as if to say, "You know, this guy's not bad."

When the defendant finished singing the chorus, he told the court, "Now this next part is the bridge between the chorus and the second verse. I don't have a guitar, but it goes like this." He then strummed an imaginary guitar with his hands and started to mimic out loud the twangy tune of the bridge the way he imagined it sounded on the guitar:

"Deer-deer-deer-dah-dah-deer-deer-de-er—"

The judge abruptly broke in on the defendant's song, and told him, "No, don't do that 'Deer-deer-deer' stuff, because the court reporter can't take that down for the record." Laughter rocked the courtroom as the defendant graciously offered to sing the rest of his song to the court.

"No thanks, that's enough singing," replied the judge. "Is there anything further from either counsel?" The judge then proceeded with the sentencing hearing.

For a number of years afterward, I mistakenly thought that the judge had sentenced the defendant to serve a term of thirty-three months in federal prison, in accordance with the joint sentencing recommendation in the defendant's negotiated plea agreement. I remember leaving the courtroom that morning feeling a twinge of sadness that the judge had not been moved to cut the defendant a break for his singing in court. I remember thinking, why not give the defendant a little credit based on something—maybe creativity, showmanship, sheer chutzpah, sincere expression of remorse, expressed commitment to rehabilitation, comic relief, or perhaps a whimsical combination of these factors? In the great scheme of things, what difference would a small sentencing reduction make with regard to the defendant's likelihood of re-offending?

The defendant had never come right out and asked the judge for less time than the joint sentencing recommendation, but it seemed perfectly reasonable to me that he was hoping to move the judge to mercy with his song. The defendant, however, was by no means a first-time offender. Banking on pure, unadulterated hope, the defendant was kind of like a panhandler asking for money on a street corner, or a musician playing for tips on the sidewalk.

As time passed, whenever I recalled the case of the singing defendant, I figured that my twinge of sadness about how his sentence had turned out was just wishful thinking on my part. I was privileged to work in this judge's courtroom many times over a period spanning more than twenty years. I always had the sense that he was a just and merciful man. If and when he erred, he erred on the side of mercy and forbearance. I think he instinctively knew that knee-jerk condemnation and harsh punishment were the easy way out. Somehow, through an unending assembly line of poor, dissembling defendants, he had the humility and empathy to see the good in people despite their transgressions. So, if the judge had seen fit not to reduce the defendant's sentence in appreciation of his singing, the judge knew perfectly well what he was doing.

When I stopped and thought about it, I realized that I myself don't give cash to panhandlers or to sidewalk musicians all the time because there are too many of them. If I gave them all my money, would I be in the same boat as them? God forbid, I might have to resort to smuggling aliens or avocados, booze or birds, iodine or iguanas, cigarettes or cigars or who knows what else to get by. "There but for the grace of God go I."

Years later, I had the opportunity to reminisce with another member of the court staff who was also in court that morning during the memorable sentencing hearing of the singing defendant. This former co-worker recalled that hearing quite distinctly. He told me in no uncertain terms that the judge *had* in fact reduced the defendant's sentence by a couple of months in recognition of his creative efforts. I don't know how I got the mistaken impression that he hadn't, but I was pleasantly surprised to find out that I was wrong.

May you rest in peace from your long labors in the service of justice, Your Honor. As you yourself would often say to me at the end of the day's calendar, "*Vaya con Dios*." ("Go with God.")

9. The Defendant Who Had His Cake and Ate It Too

"The number of fools is infinite." –Ecclesiastes 1:15

I was once assigned to interpret for a jury trial of a young man who was accused in a two-count indictment of importation of marijuana into the United States from Mexico, and possession of marijuana with the intent to distribute it. The defendant was a tall, well-built, good-looking, young resident of Tijuana who had been raised and educated on both sides of the US-Mexico border. As a result of his bilingual, bicultural upbringing, he understood and spoke English and Spanish fluently. Ironically, at the time of his arrest for drug smuggling, he was employed as a police officer for the city of Tijuana, assigned to traffic enforcement. While engaged in the performance of his official duties, he had found that his excellent command of English came in handy whenever he had the occasion to provide assistance to the numerous American tourists who visited Tijuana in those days. Whether he found himself giving helpful directions to lost tourists, or occasionally pocketing convenient cash payments for routine traffic infractions, the young officer took genuine pride in his superior abilities to serve the needs of the public in two languages.

Because he spoke English and Spanish as well as he did, it seemed odd to me at the time that he chose to use the services of the court interpreter for his trial. Nevertheless, that is what he chose to do, and that explains why my colleague and I happened to be in the courtroom to interpret his sworn testimony for the jury. Thinking about it after all these years, he may have chosen to testify in Spanish simply because he felt more comfortable speaking Spanish than English—particularly because he found himself enmeshed in risky legal proceedings in which everything that he said could be used against him. Indeed, everything that he said at his trial was ultimately used against him with devastating effect. In this way, figuratively speaking, the defendant was not entirely dissimilar to an ant blasted at point-blank range by a bazooka.

It may also be that the defendant chose to testify in Spanish so that his Spanish-speaking relatives who attended the trial could hear firsthand how unscrupulous drug smugglers had tricked him into crossing their marijuana into the United States without him having the slightest inkling that there were over 200 pounds of it hidden directly beneath his feet. Perhaps for him, particularly given his employment as a police officer, it was a way of saving face with his loved ones, or perhaps it was part of a last-ditch effort to save his job.

It is also possible that he had realized sometime during the proceedings in his case that by testifying through the interpreter, he would have a little more time—time to decide how best to answer the prosecutor's pointed questions on cross-examination. After all, even if you are testifying in English, and you haven't figured out how to answer a question without torpedoing your own ship, a time-honored, well-established stalling tactic is to say, "I didn't understand. Please repeat the question." When you are testifying through an interpreter, there seems to be no limit to the number of times you can get away with this ploy. After all, who is to say if the witness is merely a blockhead, or if the interpreter is incompetent? God help us if both things are true! Nevertheless, when used and abused as a means of evading the question, this response does have its risks. Eventually, the court's and jury's patience start to wear thin. They grow weary of hearing the same questions repeated over and over again. It becomes painfully obvious that the defendant is trying very hard not to answer certain questions, and one can only wonder why. Leaving aside the high probability that the young police officer was in fact guilty from his head to his toes—let alone devious and woefully misguided—he was by no means a stupid young man. He may have hoped that the extra bit of "breathing room" that he gained by testifying through the court interpreter would better position him to steer his testimony in the most favorable direction for his defense.

On the day of his arrest, the defendant had entered the United States from Mexico through the San Ysidro border crossing. He was the driver and sole occupant of a small, late-model Volkswagen sedan. The defendant had chosen to cross the border during the heavy weekday morning traffic of border crossers heading to work in the United States. Right from the get-go, the first inspector who encountered the defendant had noticed something out of the ordinary about the car the defendant was driving.The inspector testified that he seemed to recall that when the car rolled to a stop next to his primary inspection booth, the driver's window was already open, and the driver was already holding his legitimate border crosser document in his outstretched hand. The inspector explained that he could not recall these initial details with complete certainty, because the very first thing he noticed as the vehicle pulled alongside his booth was that the driver's knees were sticking up above the level of the bottom of the driver's window frame. He observed that the way in which the driver's knees were sticking up made him look like he was too tall to fit in the driver's seat.

"The way he was sitting reminded me of the way adults look when they drive those miniature Autopia cars at Disneyland," the inspector testified. Because the customs inspector had received extensive classroom and on-the-job training in locating hidden compartments in vehicles, he leaned forward and looked down at the floorboard underneath the driver's feet. The inspector instantly noticed that the front floorboard of the vehicle was several inches higher than normal, which explained why the defendant's knees were visible above the bottom of the window frame of the driver's door. The inspector testified that he immediately suspected that the floor of the vehicle might have been modified to accommodate contraband.

He then testified that prior to referring the vehicle to secondary inspection, he had asked the defendant a series of routine questions. He asked the driver in English what his citizenship was, to which the driver replied in English, "Mexican." He asked the driver if he had any items of merchandise to declare, to which the driver replied that he had nothing. Next, the inspector asked the driver to whom the vehicle belonged, to which the driver replied that it belonged to a friend of his who had loaned it to him while his own car was being repaired. The inspector then asked the driver what his friend's name was and noted that the driver hesitated briefly before shrugging his shoulders, smiling nervously, and answering that he just knew his friend by the nickname "Flaco" (meaning "Skinny" in English). The inspector next asked the driver to show him the registration for the vehicle. The inspector testified that the defendant opened the glove compartment, glanced inside, then looked at the inspector and told him, "I guess it's not there." Finally, the inspector asked the driver where he was going, to which the driver replied that he was going to a Pep Boys store to look for auto parts.

The inspector testified that he then filled out a referral slip, placed it on the Volkswagen's windshield underneath the windshield wiper blade, and told the driver to drive the vehicle into the secondary inspection lot and park it in one of the empty spaces. On the referral slip, the inspector had written a brief note to the effect that the front floor of the vehicle was too high, and that the secondary inspector should request an inspection by the narcotics detector dog.

In the order in which they were called, the rest of the prosecution's witnesses were: the narcotics detector dog handler, who testified that his dog had indeed alerted to the presence of a narcotic odor emanating from the front floorboard area of the vehicle; the customs inspector who had inspected the Volkswagen in the secondary lot and discovered the marijuana; another customs inspector who had been asked to serve as interpreter for the defendant's post-arrest interview; and one of the special agents from the customs service who had interviewed the defendant in

English on the day of his arrest. Thankfully, the prosecution and the defense had eliminated the need to call an expert forensic chemist by agreeing or stipulating to his testimony. The stipulation, which the prosecutor read aloud to the jury, was to the effect that based on the results of three standard tests performed by a qualified DEA forensic chemist on the samples of the substance seized from the car driven by the defendant on the day of his arrest, the substance was indeed marijuana, a Schedule 1 controlled substance. The parties also stipulated that based upon the expert opinion of a highly experienced special agent from the DEA, the large amount of marijuana seized from the Volkswagen driven by the defendant was an amount intended for distribution (rather than for strictly personal use), and that around the time of the defendant's arrest, the seized marijuana's wholesale value in the adjoining San Diego community was well in excess of $50,000.

The secondary inspector testified that he had approached the driver, asked him to step out of the vehicle, hand him the keys, and stand nearby—all of which the defendant did. He then looked at the referral slip placed on the Volkswagen's windshield by the primary inspector. He glanced at the floor, which looked abnormally high to him also. Immediately, he signaled to a nearby canine enforcement officer to bring his narcotics detector dog over and screen the vehicle. The secondary inspector testified that while waiting for the dog handler to bring his dog over to the Volkswagen, he also asked the driver if he had any articles of merchandise to declare, to which the driver had again replied that he did not.

According to the secondary inspector's testimony, as soon as the dog handler approached the Volkswagen with his dog and opened the driver's door, the dog immediately put his two front paws on the floor in front of the driver's seat. The dog then began scratching and biting at the floor mat. The dog handler looked at the secondary inspector and nodded "yes," which the secondary inspector took to mean that the dog had positively alerted to the presence of a narcotics odor inside the Volkswagen.

The secondary inspector testified that he next escorted the driver inside the security office of the secondary inspection lot, where he had the driver empty the contents of his pockets and place them on the counter. He then patted the driver down to make sure the driver had no weapons or contraband secreted on his person, which the defendant did not. He then asked the driver to take a seat on a bench inside the office and wait while the secondary inspection of the Volkswagen was being conducted outside. The driver sat down on the bench, and the secondary inspector went back outside to conduct his inspection.

The secondary inspector testified that as soon as he lifted up the floor mat beneath the driver's seat, he saw what looked like an access panel made of sheet metal and held in place with screws. The inspector testified that he then lifted up the floor mat on the front passenger side and saw that the access panel extended over most of the front floorboard of the vehicle. Using a handy screwdriver, which he found in the glove compartment of the Volkswagen, the inspector removed the screws and lifted out the access panel. There, in plain view, was a set of tightly wrapped, tightly compressed packages containing what looked like a green, leafy substance. The floor of the Volkswagen had indeed been modified to accommodate contraband. The hollow space in which the packages were hidden occupied the entire front floorboard area of the car.

The inspector used a pocketknife to cut a small opening in one of the packages. He then removed a tiny sample of the green, leafy substance, and used a field test kit to perform a preliminary chemical test of the sample. The sample tested positive for THC, the active ingredient in marijuana. The secondary inspector went on to testify how he had notified the secondary lot supervisor that he had discovered a load of marijuana, so that the lot supervisor could notify the special agents whose duty it was to assume responsibility for the follow-up investigation of narcotics seizures.

The secondary inspector had then gone back inside the security office, handcuffed the driver, and escorted him to a holding cell. Once he removed the handcuffs from the driver and secured him inside the holding cell, he picked up a camera and went back outside to the Volkswagen. He took pictures of the now-visible packages of marijuana on the front floorboard. He then removed the packages, counted, weighed, and piled them on a table in the security office. He photographed the pile of packages, secured them in the office, and went back outside to complete his inspection of the load vehicle. Aside from the contraband and the screwdriver, the secondary inspector found nothing else in the Volkswagen. Apart from the screwdriver, the glove compartment was empty. There was no registration document, no proof of insurance—no paperwork whatsoever in the car.

The next inspector the prosecutor called to the witness stand testified very briefly and was not cross-examined at all by the defense attorney. The inspector testified that on the day of the defendant's arrest, the shift supervisor had called him into the security office and had asked him to serve as interpreter for the defendant's post-arrest interview. As it happened, as soon as he had finished reading the Spanish-language version of the Miranda rights to the defendant, the defendant told him that he did not need an interpreter because he spoke English and Spanish. The case agent then re administered the Miranda rights to the defendant in English, after which the defendant waived his rights and agreed to answer questions without an attorney present. The remainder of the defendant's post-arrest interview was conducted entirely in English. It so happened that the case agent's partner agent had been required to leave the interview room for a while to attend to other business. For this reason, the case agent had asked the inspector to remain as a witness to the interview.

The case agent was the last and final witness called by the prosecutor during the presentation of his case-in-chief. The case agent and his partner had been the duty agents on the day of the defendant's arrest.

According to the case agent's testimony, he and his partner had received the call from the shift supervisor at the port of entry where the inspectors had discovered and seized the marijuana from the Volkswagen. Shortly thereafter, they had gone to the port of entry to assume responsibility for the investigation of the case. After talking to the inspectors at the port of entry and inspecting the Volkswagen and the marijuana, the two special agents sought to interview the defendant. They entered the holding cell where the secondary inspector had left the defendant. They introduced themselves to the defendant and identified themselves as federal police officers. They informed the defendant that he was under arrest for importation of marijuana into the United States, handcuffed him and removed him from the holding cell, and escorted him to an interview room. In the interview room, the special agents sat down at a table with the defendant. They removed his handcuffs, advised him of his constitutional rights, and asked him if he was willing to answer questions without an attorney present. According to the case agent, the defendant told them that he understood his rights, and because he had nothing to hide, he was happy to answer their questions.

According to the case agent's testimony, he had asked the defendant to explain how he had come to drive the Volkswagen through the port of entry earlier that morning. In summary fashion, the case agent testified that the defendant had given him the following explanation: The entire chain of events started because the defendant's own car had been having mechanical problems, and he had taken the car to an auto repair shop in Tijuana. There the mechanic diagnosed the problem and told the defendant that he could fix the car, but that would need a number of parts to complete the repairs. As the defendant's car was drivable, the mechanic told him that he could leave the car, or he could bring it back to the shop when the parts were available. According to the defendant, he had been concerned that his car might break down on the road, so he decided to leave the car at the shop and took a taxi back to his home.

The defendant told the case agent that several days had passed, and he had not heard back from the mechanic, so he had gone back to the shop to find out what was happening with his car. According to the defendant's post-arrest statement, the mechanic apologized for the delay and explained that he had not been able to get the parts in Tijuana to fix the defendant's car. The mechanic asked the defendant if he had papers to cross over to the United States, because if he did, then the defendant might be able to go to an auto parts store or a junkyard on the US side of the border and buy the necessary parts himself. According to the defendant, he told the mechanic that he was willing to go look for the parts himself in order to speed the repair job along, but he had no car to drive.

Just then, as luck would have it, a man who happened to be standing nearby at the auto repair shop offered the defendant the use of his car, if the defendant would do him the favor of buying some repair parts that he also happened to need. According to the defendant, the mechanic introduced this man to him by the nickname "Flaco." The defendant told the case agent that he had first seen Flaco the first time he had gone to the shop. Flaco seemed to be a friend of the mechanic. The defendant explained to the case agent that he needed to get his car fixed as soon as possible, and that Flaco seemed like a decent chap, so he accepted Flaco's offer.

Because the defendant was free that afternoon, he thought he might just head across the border right then to look for the repair parts. To his disappointment, Flaco told him that his car wasn't available yet, that his wife was using it, but that the defendant could return the next day and take the car. The defendant happened to have the next day off, so he agreed. (The next day turned out to be the ill-fated day of the defendant's arrest.)

The defendant went on to explain to the case agent that when he returned to the auto repair shop the next morning, Flaco was there and had given him the keys to a small, late-model Volkswagen. This Volkswagen, according to the defendant, was the car that he had driven through the port of entry, and which, unbeknown to him, had turned out to be loaded with marijuana. When Flaco gave the keys to the defendant, he told him that he had already gotten the auto parts that he himself needed, but he encouraged the defendant to go ahead and take the car as they had agreed.

According to the defendant, Flaco asked him which auto parts store the defendant was planning to go to first. Flaco's question had struck the defendant as strange, because Flaco supposedly no longer needed repair parts for himself. Flaco had also given the defendant a cell phone to use, which the defendant explained he had also thought a little strange. Supposedly, Flaco wanted to be able to get in touch with the defendant just in case he needed him to pick up some parts after all. According to the defendant, this explained why he had a cell phone in his possession, which he said did not belong to him and which rang repeatedly during the hours following his arrest. As the case agent testified, he had tried to answer the load car driver's cell phone on several occasions, but it seemed to him that whoever was calling kept hanging up as soon as they heard his voice.

The defendant told the case agent that he had driven the Volkswagen straight to the border from the auto repair shop. He had noticed that the floor seemed to be a little high, but he hadn't given it much thought. He concluded his explanation by telling the case agent that he never once suspected as he drove Flaco's Volkswagen toward the border that his feet were resting directly on top of more than 200 pounds of marijuana. After all, as the defendant explained to the case agent, he was a police officer himself and was well aware that trafficking in illegal narcotics was a serious criminal offense, not to mention dishonest and immoral. He told the case agent that he himself had received commendations from his department for his community service work as part of an anti-drug campaign targeting the youth of Tijuana, and that he would never have knowingly smuggled illegal narcotics into the United States.

According to the case agent, he had listened carefully to the defendant's explanation, and had made notes of the salient points. When the defendant finished, the case agent asked the defendant if he was saying that Flaco was responsible for the marijuana, and that Flaco had set him up. The defendant replied that he thought that Flaco must be responsible for the marijuana, and that he had indeed set him up. The case agent then asked the defendant if he was sure if his explanation of how he had come to drive the marijuana-laden vehicle was the truth. The defendant insisted it was the truth. The case agent then told the defendant that he did not believe him, and that it would be better for the defendant to tell the truth.

The defendant asked the case agent why he did not believe him. The case agent told him that for one thing, to judge by the defendant's story, it did not sound like Flaco had a very well-thought-out, reliable plan to swoop down and unload the marijuana from the car while the defendant was busy looking for auto parts in the United States. In other words, to follow the logic of the defendant's story through to its conclusion, if the defendant had bought his auto parts and returned to Tijuana as planned, there would evidently have been little or no opportunity for Flaco to unload the marijuana. Flaco would practically have had to surreptitiously follow the defendant across the border, wait for his chance, and make off with his Volkswagen while the defendant was not around. Who knew what the unsuspecting defendant might have done if he had come out of an auto parts store and had found the car missing? What if he had called the police to report a stolen car? Since Flaco would quite possibly have been unable to get his marijuana unloaded, the very same marijuana that had just been successfully smuggled north into the United States would have been very counterproductively smuggled south into Tijuana once again. As the case agent explained to the defendant, if the object of drug smuggling is to successfully sneak illegal narcotics under the noses of the border inspectors and transport them safely to their destination in the United States, then the defendant's explanation made it sound like Flaco had a very poorly thought out plan to have his marijuana smuggled into the

United States.

The defendant listened to the case agent voice his skepticism about his explanation. According to the case agent, the defendant then asked him, “If you don’t believe me, what do you want me to tell you?” The case agent testified that he had replied, “The truth. No more lies. The truth.” He reported that the defendant then told him he did not want to answer any more questions without an attorney present, and the interview was terminated.

Upon completion of the case agent’s direct examination and cross-examination, the prosecutor rested his case. After a brief recess, the defense then called the defendant as its one and only witness. Because the defendant happened to testify almost immediately after the case agent, the jury had an exceptionally good opportunity to compare and contrast the two somewhat different versions of the defendant’s explanation of how he had come to drive the marijuana-laden vehicle through the port of entry on the day of his arrest.

By and large, while answering his attorney’s questions on direct examination, the defendant recounted the same series of events that he had told the case agent. By the time of his trial, however, several months had passed. After his arrest, the defendant had been unable to post bail and, consequently, had remained in custody pending his trial. Therefore, he had had several months to sit and think long and hard about things. Evidently, driven by a burning desire to convince the jury of his innocence, the defendant had carefully sifted the facts surrounding his arrest through the fine sieve of memory, and had kneaded them with the loving care of a master baker. Like a cook intent on improving a recipe, the defendant had revised his original version. The result of his efforts was an unmistakably different creation. Thus, listening to the defendant’s trial testimony very shortly after listening to the case agent’s trial testimony about the same events was an oddly disjointed experience. It was something akin to the feeling one might get from watching two out-of-sync, poorly edited versions of the same film projected side by side on a giant television screen.

On the day of his arrest, for example, the defendant had been unable to describe to the case agent the precise location or even the street on which the auto repair shop where he supposedly had taken his own car for repairs was located. He had told the case agent the name of the neighborhood where the shop was, and that he knew how to get there, but that he could not remember the directions clearly enough to explain them to the agent. Given that the defendant was a traffic enforcement officer in Tijuana, his faulty memory about the whereabouts of the auto repair shop was a bit suspect. Then, during his trial testimony, the defendant told the jury that after his arrest, he had managed to describe to his attorney and his family how to get to the auto repair shop. Ruefully, he told the jury that when his family had gone to the location he had described, the shop was no longer there.

On the day of his arrest, the defendant told the case agent that he noticed that the floor of Flaco's car looked a bit higher than usual, but that he hadn't thought twice about it. During his trial testimony, the defendant told the jury that he had noticed that the floor of the car looked too high, and in fact he had asked Flaco about it. He said that Flaco had told him that the floor of the car had gotten soaked while passing through a rain-flooded street, and that he had had it replaced. The defendant explained to the jury that since Flaco seemed friendly and trustworthy to him, he had taken his explanation at face value and had paid no more attention to the raised floor. In response to a question by his attorney, the defendant emphatically stated that at no time did he suspect that Flaco had modified the floor of the car in order to smuggle drugs across the border.

According to the defendant's testimony at trial, on the day of his arrest, he had also regrettably neglected to mention to the case agent that he had actually crossed the border two days before in Flaco's Volkswagen. On that occasion, he said the floor of Flaco's car looked exactly the same to him as it had on the second, fateful occasion when he had crossed the border. Nevertheless, according to the defendant, on the occasion of his prior crossing, the primary inspector had waved him through the port of entry without incident. He told the jury that because he had crossed the border two days before in the same vehicle without even being sent to secondary inspection, he had even less reason to be suspicious about Flaco or his car. The defendant's attorney asked the defendant for what purpose he had made the prior crossing in Flaco's car, and the defendant answered that he had also gone to look for repair parts on that occasion, but he had been unable to find them. Then the attorney asked him why he had not told the case agent about his prior crossing in that car. The defendant shook his head regretfully, shrugged his shoulders, looked apologetically at the members of the jury, and told them in English, "I got nervous, because I had never been arrested before, and I completely forgot to tell the case agent. I apologize to him, because I wanted to help him investigate Flaco for setting me up, and you know when you are innocent, you have nothing to fear."

On the day of the defendant's arrest, the case agent had asked the defendant what repair parts he had been coming to the United States to buy, and for what make and model of car. The defendant told the case agent that his own car was a late-model Ford Mustang, and that he himself didn't know much about cars. For this reason, the defendant explained, the mechanic had given him a written list of the parts that he needed to buy. Prior to interviewing the defendant, the case agent had also inspected the Volkswagen and had taken a look at the defendant's personal belongings. The case agent had found nothing resembling such a list. Consequently, he asked the defendant where the list was. The defendant looked stricken, and replied lamely, "You mean the list is not in the car? I thought it was in the car when I crossed the border. Maybe I left it back at the auto repair shop." The case agent then asked the defendant what kind of repairs his own car needed. The defendant thought for a minute and told the case agent that his car needed a smog check, a scheduled servicing, and that the car had been overheating. When the case agent asked the defendant how he could have a mechanic in Tijuana perform a California state-mandated smog check, the defendant told him that he wasn't planning to have the Tijuana mechanic perform that task—just the other repairs.

I interpreted for the defendant during his trial testimony. Right from the start, the defendant began to answer his attorney's questions instantly, without waiting for me to interpret them into Spanish. He would answer some questions in English and others in Spanish. Soon, it was obvious to the judge, the jury, and everyone in the courtroom that the defendant understood and spoke English quite well. In such situations, one naturally wonders why the witness is testifying in Spanish if he apparently understands and speaks English perfectly. It raises a question about whether the witness honestly needs the services of the court interpreter, or whether he is monkeying around. Needless to say, such a question does not tend to foster a favorable impression in the minds of the jury about the witness's truthfulness and believability.

Fortunately, the judge presiding over the defendant's trial was anything but ineffectual. Almost immediately, he intervened to remedy the situation. First, the judge asked the defendant if he in fact spoke Spanish and English fluently, to which the defendant replied yes. Then the judge asked the defendant if he preferred to testify in Spanish, to which the defendant replied that he did. The judge then instructed the defendant to stick to Spanish, and also to wait for the interpreter to finish interpreting the questions into Spanish before answering them. The defendant smiled sheepishly, mumbled in Spanish that he was nervous because he had never been arrested before, and said "I'm sorry" in English to the judge and jury.

So onward we went with his direct examination. For a few minutes, the defendant followed the court's instructions, and his testimony flowed more smoothly. All too soon, however, the defendant reverted to answering some questions in English and others in Spanish. Once again, he started answering his attorney's questions without waiting for me to finish interpreting them into Spanish for him. Once again, the court admonished the defendant to stop mixing languages, and to wait for the questions to be interpreted into Spanish before answering them. Once again, the defendant lamely apologized in English to the judge and jury. At long last, with many lurching stops and starts along the way, and with many repetitions of the same questions, we arrived at the dramatic pinnacle of the defendant's defense.

Throughout his direct testimony, the defendant wasted no opportunity to tell the jury that he was innocent because prior to his arrest, he had never known that there was marijuana in the Volkswagen that he had driven across the border. Finally, his attorney asked the defendant point-blank: "Mr. Fonseca, when was the very first time you found out that there was marijuana in the car that you had driven into the United States that morning?"

The defendant then testified in Spanish that the very first time he found out there was marijuana hidden in the car was while he was sitting on the bench in the security office at the port of entry. This was the bench where the secondary inspector had left him waiting while he conducted his inspection outside. According to the defendant, while he was sitting on the bench, two customs inspectors entered the security office from the secondary inspection area outside. The inspectors had passed within earshot, and he overheard some of their conversation. The defendant's attorney then asked the defendant to tell the court and jury what he heard one inspector say to the other inspector. In reply, the defendant looked at me, then looked over his shoulder at the judge, and asked ever so politely in Spanish, "*¿Puedo usar malas palabras*?" which I translated as: "May I use bad words?" The court did not answer the defendant's question, and the defendant's attorney said, "Please continue, Mr. Fonseca."

The defendant then testified that he had overheard one inspector remark to the other, "*Agarramos a otro pendejo con mota*."

As it happens, in the magnificently expressive Spanish spoken in Mexico, the pejorative term "*pendejo*" is extremely common. Depending on how, when, and where it is used, it might be translated as: idiot, fool, stupid, jerk, dumb, asshole, etc. One of the very common idiomatic expressions in which "*pendejo*" is used is "*hacerse pendejo*," or "*no te hagas pendejo*," which might be translated as "to act stupid," or "don't act stupid/play dumb." This is the sort of expression that an investigating officer might use while engaged in the interrogation of an evasive, dissimulating suspect. Anyway, I translated the defendant's testimony as: "We caught another idiot with pot."

To my surprise, the defendant turned in the witness chair to look at me, and said in excellent English, "No, 'asshole.'"

In that moment, I realized that the "bad word" the defendant had asked permission to use in the presence of the court and jury was "asshole." So, I dutifully repeated in English the defendant's correction of my translation for the jury: "No, 'asshole.'"

Oddly enough, although the defendant corrected my translation, nobody ever followed up to ask him whether he was claiming to have overheard a remark made in English or a remark made in Spanish. If, as was apparently the case, the defendant was purporting to quote a remark that he had overheard one inspector make in Spanish to another inspector, then he was apparently exercising his prerogative to have "*pendejo*" translated from Spanish into English exactly as he thought it should be translated. After all, "asshole" is more offensive and inflammatory than "idiot." As a derogatory term used by a policeman to refer to a suspect, "asshole" may express the cynical, "they're-all-guilty" attitude of the border inspectors more graphically than "idiot." Since the defendant had chosen to testify, the success of his defense depended to a large extent on his ability to convince the jury that he was really an innocent dupe, notwithstanding the suspicious observations and cynical attitudes and beliefs of the federal police officers. If, on the other hand, the defendant chose to translate into Spanish a remark that he had heard the inspector make in English, then he was apparently correcting my translation *back into English* of a remark that he himself had heard spoken aloud *in English* to begin with! If that were the case, one might reasonably ask yet again, why in the world was this witness testifying in Spanish? What advantage did he hope to gain by doing so?

In either event, his correction and my dutiful repetition provoked a gust of laughter from the jury. Along with the laughter, however, it became apparent in that moment that the defendant was intent on choosing whichever language and words best suited his purposes at any given moment. He clearly wanted to be in control of his story and tell it in the light most favorable to him, which was perfectly understandable. All too soon, however, the defendant's intention would backfire.

During his cross-examination, the prosecutor carefully exposed the abovementioned inconsistencies between the statements that the defendant had made to the case agent on the day of his arrest, and the statements he had just made under oath during his direct examination. Interestingly, during his cross-examination by the prosecutor, the defendant paid far closer attention to my interpretation than he had during his direct examination. On numerous occasions, he would lean down toward me, listening intently to my interpretation. Then he would pause, and respond that he had not understood the question, and would the prosecutor please repeat it yet again.

One of the first series of questions that the prosecutor asked the defendant had to do with his choice of languages. The prosecutor asked the defendant if his entire post-arrest interview with the case agent had been conducted in English, to which the defendant replied yes. The prosecutor then asked the defendant if he had had any difficulty understanding the case agent, to which the defendant replied, "only a few times." He then asked the defendant if he had ever told the case agent that he did not understand him, or to repeat or explain his questions. The defendant said that he could not remember. The prosecutor then asked the defendant why he was testifying in court through an interpreter when he had declined to use an interpreter for his post-arrest interview. The defendant shrugged his shoulders and replied that he was nervous and wanted to be sure that he understood everything.

Perhaps the most damaging series of questions the prosecutor asked came at the very end of his cross-examination. The questions had to do with the defendant's claim that he had crossed the border in Flaco's Volkswagen sedan two days before he crossed the border in the very same car again and got arrested. The prosecutor started by asking the defendant if during his direct examination, he had in fact testified to having made the prior crossing in Flaco's car, and if he was sure that it was the same car. The defendant replied that he had indeed testified to that fact, and that he was positive it was the same car because it had the raised front floorboard. He then reiterated that the prior, uneventful crossing in Flaco's car was the reason why he had had even less cause to suspect that Flaco might be up to something illegal.

The prosecutor then showed the defendant a photograph of the load vehicle, which had previously been admitted into evidence as a government exhibit. He asked the defendant if the photograph was a fair and accurate depiction of Flaco's car on the two occasions when he had driven it across the border. The defendant replied that indeed it was. The prosecutor then asked the defendant if he was able to see the numbers of the license plate on the Volkswagen, and if so, would the defendant please read them aloud for the jury. The defendant replied that he was able to see the numbers on the license plate, and he obligingly read them aloud for the jury. The prosecutor then asked the defendant if he had happened to notice if the same license plate was on Flaco's car on both occasions when he had crossed the border in it. The defendant replied that he had not noticed if the license plate was the same or not.

After the defendant finished testifying, the defense rested its case. The prosecutor then called the case agent back to the witness stand as its one and only rebuttal witness. Over the heated objections of defense counsel, the court allowed the prosecutor to question the case agent about the computerized record the customs service keeps of vehicles crossing into the United States through land ports of entry. During pretrial preparation, the prosecutor had asked the case agent to query that computerized database in order to retrieve any history of entries into the United States by any vehicle bearing the license plate number that had been on the Volkswagen sedan driven by the defendant. The case agent had queried the database regarding that license plate number for a period of six months prior to the date of the defendant's arrest. There were numerous records of entries by the Volkswagen—or by some vehicle bearing that same license plate number—up until approximately one month prior to the date of the defendant's arrest. After that, there was no record whatsoever of any entry into the United States through the San Ysidro port of entry or any other port of entry by any vehicle having that same license plate number until the date of the defendant's arrest.

In reply to a series of questions posed by the defense attorney on cross-examination, the case agent admitted that there are times when a customs inspector might accidentally enter a license plate number incorrectly into the database. The case agent further admitted that there are times when the computer system is not working, so that there could be periods of time during which a vehicle's entry might not be duly recorded in the database. Moreover, the case agent acknowledged that the customs service computerized database does not record the identity of drivers of vehicles that enter the United States. Thus, the case agent testified that he had no personal knowledge of the identity of the person or persons who had been driving whatever vehicle had been bearing the license plate number in question on any of the prior occasions on which the customs service had a record of that vehicle's entries into the United States. Then the defense attorney asked the case agent, "So for all you know, Agent Stevens, the person driving whatever car had the license plate number that you queried could have been Flaco, the defendant, the Lone Ranger, or the Man in the Moon?" The case agent burst out laughing along with the jury, and started to nod yes in reply, when the prosecutor leapt to his feet and objected on the grounds that the question was argumentative. Before the court could rule on the objection, the defense attorney withdrew the question.

On redirect examination, the prosecutor asked the case agent if he had checked to see if the customs service computer system had been out of order at any time during the week before the defendant's arrest. The case agent replied that he had checked, and he had found no record that the system had been down at that time. In the end, the case agent's rebuttal testimony created a very strong inference that the defendant had simply made up his testimony about his first border crossing in Flaco's car. The damage to the defendant's credibility was done, and despite his attorney's determined efforts, the damage could not be undone.

Following closing arguments and the court's final instructions to the jury, the jurors withdrew to the jury room to commence their deliberations. They did not take long. Before the day was through, the jury had returned a verdict of guilty as to both charges against the defendant—that he had knowingly and intentionally imported marijuana into the United States, and that he had possessed marijuana with the intent to distribute it. The court thanked and excused the jury, and promptly set the date for the defendant's sentencing in due course. The "justice factory" was well on the way to turning out yet another unit of finished justice.

I did not happen to be assigned to that particular courtroom on the occasion of the defendant's sentencing. Long afterward, someone told me how much time the defendant had received, though I don't recall that number now or who told me—the defense attorney, prosecutor, or perhaps a probation officer. However, I recall that it was a far longer prison sentence than the one he could have received if he had accepted a plea offer and pled guilty. Instead, he exercised his constitutional right to a trial by jury. In so doing, he also exercised his constitutional right to testify instead of invoking his right to remain silent and not incriminate himself. The defendant very deliberately elected to testify. To this day, I wonder if he ever admitted to himself or anyone else that he very deliberately elected to testify falsely.

In the end, both the defendant's story and the way in which he chose to tell it were resoundingly rejected by the jury as patently unworthy of belief. He was the boy who cried wolf. He was Pinocchio. He was the defendant who had his cake and ate it too. It was a lopsided, apocryphal cake of his own making, mixed and baked ever so carefully throughout the long months when he had sat scheming in jail. Fresh out of the oven and cooling, there it sat on the defense table, a multilayered figment of his imagination with a secret pocket of pure, preposterous prevarication baked deep inside.

It was a cake that no one but the defendant could see. It was his choice and his choice alone whether to eat it. Did he ever really hesitate before taking his first bite? Did he ever once stop and ask himself if he was doing the smart thing, let alone the right thing? Only the defendant could say for sure. Once he bit into the cake, though, he buried his face in it and devoured it like a man determined to win the pie-eating contest at a county fair. Faster and faster he ate, hardly chewing, scarcely pausing to come up for air, until finally he had swallowed the whole improbable creation, right down to the last, richly implausible crumb.

10. "Dat'sa Boolshi—!"

A number of years ago, I happened to be assigned to interpret for the trial of a very angry defendant. The defendant's name was something like Eusebio Puentes de Roca. Luckily for the angry defendant—although he did not consider himself lucky at all—the court had appointed a friendly, capable, easygoing defense attorney to represent him. This defense attorney was at least twice as patient as Job, and probably could have gotten along famously with most of the great psychopaths of history if duty had required it of him. Only God knows how the attorney managed to defend Mr. Puentes de Roca at all, given the man's intractable belligerence toward anyone who had anything to do with his case. Indeed, Mr. Puentes de Roca had already "fired" his two previous court-appointed attorneys. Not surprisingly, on the eve of trial, he also asked the court to give his third and final attorney the boot. The court, however, had run out of patience with his "free-lawyer-shopping" shenanigans, and flatly denied his request.

Mr. Puentes de Roca professed to be angry for a number of reasons, which gradually became clear over the course of the proceedings in his case. Listed by apparent order of increasing intensity, Mr. Puentes de Roca's reasons were as follows. 1) He felt humiliated for having gotten caught smuggling aliens once again—that is, he was embarrassed by his own abysmal track record as a professional smuggler. 2) It galled him that his cowardly passengers had the nerve to testify against him at trial. After all, as he told his attorney, the undocumented people wanted to come to the United States. He was merely providing them with transportation on their journey to a better life. 3) He was indignant at what he saw as the trumped-up nature of the government's evidence against him. 4) He hated the Border Patrol agents for having thumped him a few times while he was diligently attempting to evade apprehension. 5) He resented the federal marshals for having provoked him and roughed him up one day while escorting him from the courtroom. To add insult to injury, the federal prosecutor then had the audacity to bring a charge of assaulting a federal officer against *him*! 6) He was incensed that the federal prosecutor earnestly desired to see him imprisoned for such a lengthy period of time, given that the defendant had never served more than a year in custody for his impressive string of prior misdemeanor and felony convictions.

His attorney had repeatedly counseled Mr. Puentes de Roca to let go of his anger at least long enough to listen to his advice, focus calmly on the evidence of the case, and attempt to make a sensible, rational decision about how best to proceed.

In the weeks prior to the commencement of trial, the defense attorney had carefully analyzed the government's evidence against the defendant. He had patiently, diligently attempted to review the evidence in the case with his client, despite Mr. Puentes de Roca's contemptuous dismissal of the so-called objective facts of the case. The defense attorney had repeatedly counseled Mr. Puentes de Roca that in his professional opinion, the most reasonable course of action was for him to plead guilty with a plea agreement that would contain a joint sentencing recommendation of twenty-four months in prison. While this was unquestionably a long sentence, it was approximately four times shorter than the sentence to which the defendant was exposing himself by going to trial instead of pleading guilty. Nevertheless, up until the time of trial and despite his attorney's best efforts to persuade him to see reason, Mr. Puentes de Roca had adamantly refused even to consider such an outrageously unfair option for settling his case.

Needless to say, it did not make the defense attorney's job any easier that during the earlier phases of Mr. Puentes de Roca's case, while he was being represented by his first and second court-appointed attorneys, the government had made him an eighteen-month offer, which Mr. Puentes de Roca had scornfully rejected. The government had long since withdrawn that better offer, and despite Mr. Puentes de Roca's repeated complaints of the government's unfair, arbitrary treatment, and his demands that his attorney bring him a better offer than twenty-four months, the eighteen-month offer was gone for good. Mr. Puentes de Roca was charged with alien smuggling. He himself was an undocumented border crosser and had prior felony and misdemeanor convictions for illegal entry and alien smuggling. At trial, the evidence the government presented against him was straightforward and seemingly incontrovertible. To begin with, after Mr. Puentes de Roca's arrest, the Border Patrol agents had detained three of the smuggled aliens whom he had picked up on the side of the freeway and had held them in custody as material witnesses in the case. The remaining smuggled passengers had been returned to Mexico.

On the day of Mr. Puentes de Roca's arrest, all three of the detained material witnesses had been shown a photographic lineup, which included a photograph of him. All three of the witnesses had unequivocally identified Mr. Puentes de Roca as the driver of the car in which they had been arrested. During the trial, all three of the witnesses once again recognized and identified the defendant sitting in the courtroom as the driver of the load vehicle. They also confirmed that on the day of their arrest, they had identified the photograph of Mr. Puentes de Roca as a photograph of the load car driver. Additionally, all three of the witnesses testified that Mr. Puentes de Roca had been present in a hotel room in Mexicali, Mexico, approximately two days before their illegal entry into the United States. On that occasion, according to the testimony of the three witnesses, they had met with Mr. Puentes de Roca along with another man. The three witnesses testified that during that meeting they had made arrangements to be smuggled into the United States, to be picked up at a prearranged place alongside the freeway in a remote, rural area of the back country, and to have relatives pay the smugglers for their safe delivery to the Los Angeles area.

To make matters worse for Mr. Puentes de Roca, and unbeknown to him, Border Patrol agents had him under surveillance when he picked up his undocumented passengers. During the trial, these agents testified that on the day of the defendant's arrest, they had been patrolling that particular stretch of interstate freeway in a marked Border Patrol vehicle, and happened to come within view of the vehicle being driven by the defendant just as it had started to pull over to the shoulder of the freeway. It was a clear, sunny morning, and the agents had an unobstructed view of the straight stretch of freeway ahead of them. Suspecting that alien smuggling might be afoot, the Border Patrol agents stopped on the shoulder of the freeway at a considerable distance behind the suspected load vehicle, and quickly reached for their binoculars.

Watching through their binoculars, the agents observed Mr. Puentes de Roca as he stopped at a seemingly random place on the shoulder of the freeway and got out of the car. The agents testified that they saw the defendant walk quickly around the car, open both of the passenger-side doors, and gesture with his hand. Within seconds, the agents observed approximately six to eight people appear from the thick brush adjacent to the shoulder of the freeway, and pile into the car as quickly as possible. The agents observed that as soon as the suspected undocumented aliens got into the car, they all ducked down out of sight below the windows of the vehicle. While they were piling into the car, Mr. Puentes de Roca also got back into the car. The agents then observed the defendant driving the now-loaded vehicle slowly along the shoulder of the freeway, and merge into the right-hand lane of traffic as soon as he could.

The agents testified that they radioed other nearby Border Patrol units to request assistance. They pulled back out onto the freeway, turned on their overhead lights and siren, and started to pursue the load vehicle. They accelerated quickly, and soon were driving close behind the vehicle the defendant was driving. The defendant paid no attention to the lights and siren. He did not slow down or pull over to the shoulder of the freeway, but instead continued driving at normal freeway speed. A refreshingly low-speed chase ensued, which lasted for less than five minutes, and which resulted in no one being injured. The agents testified that when they tried to pull alongside the load vehicle, the driver abruptly started zigzagging back and forth between the two lanes of the freeway. The driver tried to accelerate away from the Border Patrol vehicle, but evidently the vehicle he was driving was unexpectedly beset by some mechanical failure. Suddenly, the agents heard what sounded like a small explosion, and found themselves driving through a thick cloud of smoke billowing out of the load vehicle's tail pipe. The load vehicle then slowed down and veered over to the right shoulder of the freeway.

The agents testified that they too pulled their patrol vehicle over to the shoulder. As they were rolling to a stop behind the load vehicle, they saw the driver's door fly open, and the driver jump out and dash off into the bushes while the vehicle was still rolling slowly along the shoulder. The agents testified that one of the passengers riding in the front seat of the load vehicle had the presence of mind to slide behind the wheel of the car, apply the brakes, and bring it safely to a stop. All of the passengers were frightened and remained inside the car.

While one of the Border Patrol agents stayed with the load vehicle, the other Border Patrol agent pursued Mr. Puentes de Roca through the dense underbrush alongside the freeway. Assisted by other agents who soon arrived on the scene, the Border Patrol agent eventually overtook Mr. Puentes de Roca and placed him under arrest, following an impromptu sparring match which Mr. Puentes de Roca ultimately lost.

Following his arrest, and after having been advised of his constitutional rights, including his right to remain silent and not incriminate himself, he declined to answer questions without having an attorney present. Therefore, the government had no incriminating statements made by the defendant to use against him at trial. As things turned out, the government did not need any more evidence than it already had.

During his jury trial, Mr. Puentes de Roca ultimately elected not to testify in his own defense. This was somewhat amazing, given his repeated, righteous proclamations to his attorney that he was going to take the witness stand and tell the truth. He would prove to the jury how all of the government's witnesses were either mistaken in their testimony or lying through their teeth. In this way, at least, the defense attorney inexplicably managed to exert some sort of calming, sensible influence upon his client.

During the trial, it was not so much that Mr. Puentes de Roca was angry about the fix that he was in that made for a lively show, but rather the way in which he expressed his anger. At seemingly random intervals, while he sat sullenly at the defense table listening to the presentation of the government's evidence against him, he would cross his arms peevishly, shake his head like a mule, and loudly exclaim, "Dat'sa boolshi—!"

Mr. Puentes de Roca had been in and out of the United States on numerous occasions and had apparently been exposed to English long enough to have picked up a smattering of essential words and phrases. He spoke English with a heavy accent, however, which might explain why he never quite enunciated the final "t" in "bullshit." Even without the final "t," so long as one was close enough to him, there was no mistaking what the defendant was saying. Over the course of the trial, his numerous, vehement outbursts were like dramatic exclamation points scattered whimsically on an otherwise humdrum stream of insipid legal discourse.

The defense attorney and I were seated closest to Mr. Puentes de Roca. Like it or not, we were privy to each and every one of his remarks. The defense attorney tried numerous times in vain to placate his client, to calm him down and get him to stop exclaiming, "Dat'sa boolshi—!" whenever his anger got the better of him. Sometimes he would put his finger to his lips and try to shush Mr. Puentes de Roca. Other times he would keep his gaze fixed straight ahead and hold his hand up sideways to the defendant, something like a traffic control officer gesturing to an oncoming car to stop. On more than one occasion, he would sigh resignedly and would gesture to me to come over and interpret for him. I would approach the two of them and sit in a chair next to the defendant.

"Mr. Puentes de Roca," his attorney would implore him, "I have already told you that you are not making a very good impression on the jury or helping your defense at all by swearing out loud like you are doing. Please, for your own sake, stop interrupting, and quit cussing in the courtroom!"

The defendant would glare balefully at his attorney, shake his head dismissively and say things like, "What do you expect me to do, nothing? They are all lying, and I can prove it." The defense attorney would gaze wearily at the defendant and turn his attention back to the proceedings.

Fortunately for Mr. Puentes de Roca, his trial was being held in a courtroom roughly the size of a small airplane hangar. In spite of its outsized dimensions, the judge and the jury were seated in close enough proximity to the defendant that at least some of them could probably hear that from time to time, he was engaging in some sort of emphatic, disgruntled commentary about the proceedings. Whether everyone heard each and every one of the defendant's outbursts I cannot say for sure, although my guess is that they probably did not. This was partly because Mr. Puentes de Roca's decibel level rose and fell somewhat, evidently depending on the degree of contempt that he felt at any given moment toward the federal prosecutor's presentation of the government's case-in-chief.

The other reason that everyone may not have distinctly heard everything that the defendant said was that whenever he piped up, he was invariably interrupting the prosecutor and/or the witness seated on the witness stand. Because of this, whenever Mr. Puentes de Roca would cut loose with another "Dat'sa boolshi—!" everyone in the courtroom would stop talking for a second and stare curiously at him. Then the proceedings would resume, and everyone would once again turn their attention to the matter at hand, at least until the defendant's next rambunctious interjection.

The judge presiding over the trial definitely heard the defendant's outbursts more than once, because the first couple of times that he spoke out of turn, I saw the judge glance at the defendant out of the corner of her eye and then look away, as though pretending not to have heard him. Perhaps the judge was hoping that by ignoring Mr. Puentes de Roca, he would eventually cease and desist, just as parents sometimes ignore a misbehaving child. He did not cease and desist, however, and soon, following each outburst, the judge would glare disapprovingly at him, as though hoping that a stern judicial frown would be sufficient to deter the defendant from continuing to engage in his boisterous antics.

Perhaps Mr. Puentes de Roca was oblivious to the judge's dirty looks, or perhaps he just didn't give a hoot. Regardless, the defendant continued to disrupt the proceedings every so often with an emphatic "Dat'sa boolshi—!" Finally, there came a point when the judge had heard enough.

It happened when Mr. Puentes de Roca had heard either the prosecutor or a witness making reference to the date of his arrest. Mr. Puentes de Roca shoved his chair back from the defense table with a scowl, shook his head obstinately, and growled, "Dat'sa boolshi—!" yet again. The judge glared at him for an instant, then announced sweetly to the jury and the parties, "We'll take our midmorning recess at this time. Ladies and gentlemen of the jury, please remember the admonition that the court has given you previously not to discuss the case, nor to form or express any opinion about the case until it has finally been submitted to you. We'll be in recess for fifteen minutes. Will the parties please stay behind for a minute?"

The jury filed dutifully out of the courtroom while the rest of us stayed put. After the last member of the jury had left the room, the judge addressed the defendant. "Mr. Puentes de Roca," she began, as the defense attorney gestured to the defendant to stand up while being addressed by the judge. The judge then launched into a heated admonition to Mr. Puentes de Roca to the effect that each and every time he spoke out of turn, he was violating both the rules of courtroom decorum and basic civility, not to mention infringing on the government's right to a fair, orderly trial. She stated that he was not the only one entitled to a fair trial but he was the only one who was persisting in interrupting the lawyer and witnesses for the opposing side, that the court assumed that his attorney had advised him that his disruptive behavior was very likely not making a favorable impression on the members of the jury, and it was certainly not helping him present a meritorious defense to the charges. She reminded him that he had the right to testify or remain silent as he chose, but that did not mean that he could speak out of turn whenever he felt like it, and that if he persisted in making disruptive remarks, he was running a very real risk of being held in contempt of court.

While the judge was admonishing him, Mr. Puentes de Roca glared at her sullenly, but he did not interrupt. When she finished, he replied, "Yes, Your Honor, but the problem is that the witness is lying, and I can prove it!"

The judge then told Mr. Puentes de Roca that through his attorney, he had the right to confront and cross-examine all of the government's witnesses against him, as his attorney had been doing throughout the proceedings thus far. She then asked the defense attorney if he would like to take the opportunity to consult with Mr. Puentes de Roca during the remainder of the recess. He replied that he would of course be more than happy to consult with his client. The judge then left the bench, and the defense attorney asked me to interpret for his client and him.

The defense attorney asked Mr. Puentes de Roca what the government witness was lying about, and how he could prove it. Mr. Puentes de Roca replied, "He's lying about the date of my arrest. He's saying that he arrested me on May 2. Dat'sa boolshi—! He arrested me on May 1!"

The defense attorney looked despairingly at his client. "Mr. Puentes de Roca," he said, "we have gone over this again and again! Every one of the investigative reports and every one of the charging documents in your case lists the date of your arrest as May 2. Besides, I have already explained to you that the indictment against you says that you committed the crime of transportation of undocumented aliens *on or about* May 2. What's more, the judge is going to read an instruction to the jury which says that the government does not have to prove beyond a reasonable doubt that the date of the offense is exactly as alleged in the indictment, but only that the government must prove beyond a reasonable doubt that the crime was committed on a date *reasonably near* to the date alleged in the indictment. Besides, realistically, if the government can prove beyond a reasonable doubt that you illegally transported undocumented aliens, what difference does it make if you committed the crime on May 1 or May 2?"

"Dat'sa boolshi—!" replied Mr. Puentes de Roca. "Let me see a calendar!" The defense attorney rummaged through the papers on the defense table until he laid hands on a calendar. He placed the month of May in front of his client. Mr. Puentes de Roca muttered to himself as his index finger hovered menacingly over the first, defenseless days of May, gliding back and forth like a needle on a Ouija board. Finally, with a knowing nod of his head and a triumphant "Ah-hah!" his finger stabbed May 1 like a heron spearing a doomed minnow in the shallows. "You see? He's lying! He couldn't have arrested me on May 2 because I was already in jail on May 2! Dat'sa boolshi—! You ask the witness how he could have arrested me on May 2 if I was already in jail that day!"

His defense attorney stared hopelessly at Mr. Puentes de Roca. "All right, Mr. Puentes de Roca. If you want me to ask the witness that question, I will ask him."

After the recess, and as soon as the defense attorney began his cross-examination, he asked the witness if he was sure that he had in fact arrested Mr. Puentes de Roca on May 2. The witness replied that he was quite sure that he had arrested him on that day. The defense attorney then asked the witness if it was possible that he was mistaken as to the date, and if in fact he might have arrested Mr. Puentes de Roca on May 1 instead of May 2.

"No, sir, it is not possible that I am mistaken as to the date," replied the witness.

"How can you be so sure about the date of Mr. Puentes de Roca's arrest?" asked the defense attorney.

"Because I did not work on May 1, sir. I had taken some vacation time, and May 1 was the last day of my vacation. May 2 was my first day back on duty after my vacation. That is how I know for sure that I did not arrest Mr. Puentes de Roca on May 1." Shortly afterward, the defense attorney finished his cross-examination and sat down next to Mr. Puentes de Roca. He signaled to me to interpret for his client and him. When I approached them, the defense attorney leaned over to Mr. Puentes de Roca, shrugged his shoulders, and said quietly, "Well, we gave it a try. Do you still believe that you were arrested on May 1?"

Mr. Puentes de Roca glared at his attorney and grumbled, "He's lying! He could not arrest me on May 2, because I was already in jail on May 2. "Dat'sa boolshi—!"

His defense attorney stared back at him and calmly said, "If you think of anything else that you want me to ask the witnesses, just let me know, will you please? And please, please, for your own sake, quit cussing in court!" Then he turned his attention back to the next government's witness.

Regardless of how many times the attorney told the defendant that he was not making a good impression on the jury with his rude comments, or how forcefully and repeatedly the judge admonished the defendant about his remarks being disruptive, inappropriate, and harmful to his defense, the defendant kept repeating "Dat'sa boolshi—!" off and on throughout the trial. Little by little, it became the battle cry of his defense. It was his indelible, partially illegible signature on the trial, his shield and trademark, his defiant stamp of diehard denial.

The defendant's jury trial took fewer than two days from start to finish. Once the case was submitted to the jury for deliberations, the jury took very little time to return a unanimous verdict of guilty on every single count in the indictment. At the defense attorney's request, the jury was polled as to their verdict, and each and every member confirmed that he or she had found the defendant guilty as to every charge against him. As the jury was being polled, Mr. Puentes de Roca muttered under his breath, "Dat'sa boolshi—!" The judge then thanked and excused the jury; the jury left the courtroom, and the judge set the date and time for the sentencing hearing. The marshals whisked the defendant away, and everybody left the courtroom. Soon, the defense attorney and I were the last two people left in that cavernous courtroom. He was putting his files in his briefcase, and I was putting away the interpreter's audio equipment. At a certain moment, we looked at one another. He shook his head, rolled his eyes, and we both burst out laughing.

About three months later, I was assigned to that particular courtroom on the day of the defendant's sentencing. When all was said and done, and based on the federal sentencing guidelines (which were all but mandatory at the time), the defendant was sentenced to one hundred months in federal prison—slightly more than four times longer than what he might have received if he had taken his attorney's advice and pled guilty instead of going to trial. When it was Mr. Puentes de Roca's turn to address the court, he ranted for a while about the injustice of the justice system and then fell silent. While the court was imposing sentence, the defendant just stared fixedly at the floor with his arms crossed, shaking his head from time to time, and muttering under his breath. When the hearing was concluded, the marshals quickly escorted the defendant from the courtroom. His attorney barely had time to tell Mr. Puentes de Roca that he would be filing the notice of intent to appeal for him, and that he would visit him soon at the federal jail to explain the appeal process to him. For his part, Mr. Puentes de Roca had just enough time to glance contemptuously over his shoulder at his attorney and mutter indignantly, “Dis is boolshi—!” Then he was gone.

Every so often, that good-hearted defense attorney and I run into one another in the courtrooms. Almost invariably, after a few minutes, we recall the ludicrous case of Mr. Puentes de Roca and burst out laughing. We laugh until the judge enters the courtroom, the clerk calls the court to order, and we all leap to our feet respectfully. Then we all sit down, much like in church. The clerk calls the first matter on the calendar and we all assume our respective positions, like actors rehearsing a play. Each of us does our small, essential part to keep the production line of the justice factory running at maximum capacity. Days, weeks and years go by, and the plant just keeps turning out a staggering number of units of finished justice. At times, it feels as though the sheer volume of units produced per annum were the ultimate measure of our steadfast allegiance to that blindfolded figure who holds the fickle scales, silently mocking her own constitutional right to remain silent and never incriminate herself, not even before God.

11. The Face in the Glove Compartment

In honor of my friendly parking attendant,
now moved on to "greener lots."

There is no denying that jury service is a solemn obligation—an obligation that must be taken seriously. If you are called to jury duty, and you find yourself selected to decide whether or not a fellow human being has been proven guilty beyond a reasonable doubt of having committed a crime, then it goes without saying that you should not take your responsibility lightly. Serving on a jury is no laughing matter. Of course, in any given jury trial, unusual, unexpected, or even ludicrous events may occur, and people will naturally laugh in spite of their solemn surroundings. There is nothing wrong with this, because laughter is probably the best and cheapest antidote for the tedium, torpor, and glassy-eyed stupefaction that often accompany a criminal trial—particularly a long criminal trial in the course of which it becomes painfully obvious that there is no defense to the charge. In the end, however, a jury trial is not intended to be a work of comedy. Indeed, it is not a comedy in the slightest for a defendant who is ultimately found guilty by the jury, especially if the defendant turns out to be innocent, or as often happens, if the defendant is unshakably convinced that he is innocent. Nor is it a comedy, needless to say, for the defendant's loved ones, friends, and closest associates, not to mention business partners.

Having said this, the fact is that there are trials, and there are trials. Some trials involve deadly serious crimes, and other trials—however solemn they are supposed to be—turn out to involve criminal conduct that is laughable. These are trials wherein the defendant's criminal conduct is so brazen, inept, ill-advised or stupid, that all one can do is gape in amazement and laugh one's head off—provided, of course, that one laughs later on, somewhere out in the real world, far removed from the sober environs of the courtroom.

Consider, for example, a case of a would-be bank robber who tried to sneak into a bank after hours by crawling and slithering through the heating and air conditioning vents above the ceiling of the bank. The robber intended to remove the vent cover in the ceiling and drop down like a cat to the floor of the bank. Unfortunately for him, the vent shaft turned out to be a very tight fit. Undeterred, the robber kept on going, until he found himself stuck half in and half out of the vent opening in the ceiling, unable to hoist himself back up the same way he had come down or wriggle any farther downward toward the promised land. Stuck like a spud in a tailpipe, he spent a long, sleepless, and very uncomfortable night waiting for the bank to open the next day. When the bank employees arrived the next morning for work, unlocked the doors and let themselves in, they saw a pair of legs dangling from the ceiling. From time to time, the legs still flailed feebly, like a man trying vainly to run in midair, but mostly they just hung limply in abject defeat.

Photographs were taken of the robber's legs dangling from the ceiling before the good people from the fire department laboriously extracted him from his predicament. As soon as he had the welcome feel of solid ground under his feet again, the police arrested him on suspicion of attempted commercial burglary and whisked him off to jail. Initially, the defendant claimed that he had been working on the heating and air conditioning vents and had just happened to get stuck in the ceiling while diligently engaged in the performance of his duties.

Sometime later, the defendant evidently had a change of heart. Without knowing for sure, one may surmise that the would-be bank robber was given an opportunity to view the evidence gathered by the police in his case, which presumably would have included the damning photographs of his own legs dangling from the bank ceiling. To see such pictures with his own eyes might well have had a sobering effect upon the defendant.

The defendant's options, like those of all defendants, were either to plead guilty or go to trial. In the end, in spite of and perhaps also because of the considerable potential that the case had to provide comic relief to the court and jury, the defendant chose to plead guilty. Consequently, the case of the dangling bank robber did not go to trial.

People who work in the justice system sometimes say that a certain case "should not go to trial." The dangling bank robber's case was perhaps as good an example as any of just such a case. This is not because the defendant does not have the constitutionally guaranteed right to go to trial, but because sometimes, all things considered, it is clearly a better option for the defendant to negotiate a plea agreement and plead guilty. More on this below.

It was another one of these iffy kinds of cases that unexpectedly became a topic of conversation one day when I just happened to be on jury duty. Not only was I on jury duty, but I had been picked to serve as the second alternate juror. After all the years I had spent in the "justice factory," where we crank out justice like sausage, who would have thought they would have picked a hard-hearted guy like me to be a juror? It just goes to show that you never know what or who is coming down the pipe.

Being an alternate juror is very much like being a spare tire, or an insurance policy, or maybe a second-string quarterback. Unless you happen to be called on to take the place of one of the first twelve jurors, you are, for all intents and purposes, a useless appendage to the trial. As such, if fate decrees that you be picked as the *second* alternate juror, you are very much like a second spare tire, a backup insurance policy, or a third-string quarterback. In other words, you are twice as useless as the first alternate juror, or maybe even four times as useless, if viewed in exponential terms. Of course, your utter uselessness could instantaneously change to unsurpassed usefulness, if, God forbid, one of the first twelve jurors and also the first alternate juror should both happen to succumb to some sudden illness, have a serious accident, or be otherwise rendered incapacitated or unavailable to continue to serve on the jury. Thankfully, such double-barreled catastrophes do not seem to befall juries very often.

Now, despite the judges' kind advice to prospective jurors that they ought not to take it personally if they do not get picked to serve on the jury, it is plain that some people do take it personally. To judge by the startled, indignant looks on their faces when they are thanked and excused by the court, and also by the huffy way that some excused jurors exit the courtroom, it is plain that their egos have been bruised. There they were, leaning back in their seats, smugly secure in their manifest superiority as USDA Choice, prime-cut jury stock, fully expecting to serve on the jury, and then the damn lawyers yanked the rug right out from under their feet!

My guess is that for these same people, if they were to be selected for the role of second alternate juror, it might strike them as an embarrassingly insignificant, even demeaning part to play in the riveting human drama of the trial. Being an alternate juror would be beneath them; it would be like knowing what a gifted actor or actress you are, and then being picked as an anonymous extra for a crowd scene in a movie. A rinky-dink bit part, a few humiliating scraps from the sumptuous banquet table. "How dare they make me an alternate juror!"

I, however, was not bothered in the slightest by my likely uselessness as a second alternate juror, nor by my humble place in the grand scheme of things. I was glad that I had been chosen as a juror for the first time and felt proud of the juror badge pinned to my shirt pocket. There was a spring in my step as I made my way along the sun-splashed streets of downtown San Diego. The court had given us an extra-long lunch hour, and there I was, footloose and fancy-free. No tie, no briefcase, no worries. It was a fine spring day, and life was fabulous!

I was running a few errands over the lunch hour and had gone by the parking garage to pay my monthly parking fee and stow a few things in my truck. I stopped at the parking attendants' booth to hand in my check. As I stood waiting, Faye, the ever-friendly attendant happened to notice my juror badge. "Oh, so you're on jury duty?" she asked, with a sly smile.

"Yes, I am, Madame Attendant," I said, striking the most dramatic pose I could while balancing precariously on the edge of the little concrete island surrounding the booth. "I'll have you know that *I* am the second alternate juror, thank you very much! Go ahead and ask me, Faye: what does a second alternate juror actually do?"

Faye smiled and indulged me. "OK, OK, what does a second alternate juror actually *do*?" she asked, her voice practically dripping with curiosity.

I smiled back, and said, "Thank you for asking, Faye. Just think of me as a second spare tire, in case the jalopy of the jury has two blowouts along the rough, rutted road to a just and true verdict."

Faye looked me and rolled her eyes. She knew me well enough to take whatever I said with a block of salt. "Do you *want* to serve on the jury?" she asked dubiously.

"Yes, I do," I answered. "I have always been curious to know how juries reach their decisions."

"Not me," she said. "I don't want to serve."

"Well, there is a difference between serving on a jury in the superior court and serving on a jury in the federal court, where I work," I said. "I mean, in the superior court you are dealing with violent crimes day in and day out—murder, rape, armed robbery, assaults, mayhem, domestic violence, carjacking, child abuse. Terrible stuff. Over in federal court, they are crimes too, but it's usually a matter of how many pounds of pot you have stashed in the trunk or how many undocumented aliens you have hidden under a rug. I mean they are crimes, and once in a while we'll get a serious crime of violence, but for the most part, you can't compare the crimes we see in federal court to the crimes you see in superior court."

I guess my mention of alien smuggling rang a bell in my parking attendant's memory. Maybe Faye herself had served on a jury trial involving alien smuggling, or perhaps she knew someone else who had served on the jury in such a trial, and that person had described their impressions to her. Anyway, I was surprised when Faye shook her head, and said, "Stuffing a poor lady in a glove compartment!" Then she started to laugh.

I started to laugh too, and pompously corrected her: "Excuse me, Faye. You mean stuffing a poor lady inside the *dashboard*. So far, I haven't seen anybody quite small enough to fit entirely inside a glove compartment."

Faye kept on laughing. "How do they get them in there?" she asked curiously.

I kept on laughing too. "They loosen up the supports of the dashboard and lift it up. Then they have the person shoehorn their body inside the space, close the dashboard back up, and off they go! USA or bust!"

Faye seemed aghast at the prospect of being transported within such a confined space in the innards of a motor vehicle. She shuddered involuntarily and exclaimed, "They're not gettin' me in there!" She was still laughing as she turned her attention to a customer leaving the lot.

I, too, was still laughing as I rode the elevator up to my parking level and dropped my things off in my truck. Before I closed and locked the door, I looked suspiciously at the dashboard for a second. Faye's words came back to me, and I burst out laughing again as I took the stairs back down to the street level. Faye was still inside the booth. I approached her, and she started laughing again. I asked her, "Can you imagine opening a glove compartment in a car, peering in there, and seeing a face staring back at you? Who's more scared, the inspector who opens the glove box and sees the face in there, or the undocumented person who is crammed inside the dashboard, and staring out at the inspector?"

We both started laughing again. Faye shook her head again and repeated, "They're not gettin' me in there! No way!"

"See you later, Faye," I said, and headed back out into the fine spring day. I was still laughing as I made my way back to the courthouse.

By the way, the jury trial on which I was serving at the time had nothing to do with alien smuggling. If it had been a trial involving charges of transportation of undocumented aliens or some similar offense, I would never have talked about the facts of the case or even those of a similar case with my friendly parking attendant. Notwithstanding my jaded sense of humor, I know that when one is serving as a trial juror, it is never right to let the facts and circumstances of one case influence one's judgment in another case.

In all fairness, is the crime of secreting an undocumented foreign national inside the dashboard of my own car, and then attempting to smuggle that individual into the United States by driving my car through a port of entry without declaring to the customs inspector that I have a person hidden inside my dashboard (i.e., alien smuggling via dashboard) one of the kinds of criminal cases that some people say "should not go to trial?" After all, how plausible is it that I am driving my own car across the border with a live human being hidden inside the dashboard, and I truly haven't the slightest idea that said live human being is literally hiding right under my nose? If I honestly do not know that the person is hiding there, how and when is the person supposed to get out? In such a scenario, a very dangerous situation could potentially have a tragic outcome.

Moreover, let's say that I was even present and complicit when the person was placed inside my dashboard. Maybe I myself placed the person inside my dashboard, and I then attempted to smuggle the person into the United States. Let's say that I ended up getting caught, arrested, and prosecuted. I knowingly committed each of the essential elements of the offense of transportation of an undocumented alien. I am guilty, plain and simple, and I know that I am guilty.

Assuming all of the foregoing, do I have any moral obligation to "do the right thing," plead guilty to the charge, and sincerely accept responsibility for my illegal actions? If I decide to plead not guilty to the indictment against me, if I choose to exercise my right to a jury trial, and I do go to trial, knowing full well that in truth I am guilty as charged, does my very act of going to trial constitute an act of dishonesty and evasion of responsibility? Am I not trying to fool the judge and jury? After all, no one likes to have the wool pulled over their eyes. These are the kinds of questions that I came to ask myself about the so-called "dashboard cases" I had seen as an interpreter in the courts over the years. As a general rule, it seems to me that as human beings we ought to do the right thing and be accountable for our actions. When we make a mistake or do something wrong, we should own up to it, should we not?

At the same time, I understand that my personal notions of moral accountability have nothing to do with the bedrock rights and choices of a defendant in a criminal case. Whether I am guilty or innocent, the Bill of Rights establishes that I have the right to go to trial and hold the government to its burden of proving my guilt beyond a reasonable doubt to the unanimous satisfaction of a jury of twelve of my peers. It's that simple, and it's that flat-out profound.

What's more, each and every one of us, if accused of a crime, also has the right to be presumed innocent unless and until we are proven guilty, the right to be represented by qualified, competent defense counsel, and to have said counsel appointed to represent us if we cannot afford to pay for legal representation. If we elect to plead not guilty and go to trial, we have the right at trial to confront and cross-examine adverse witnesses, the right to challenge the admissibility of the government's evidence against us, and the right to present an affirmative defense (i.e., to subpoena our own witnesses and to present exculpatory testimony and evidence). Perhaps most valuable of all among these rights, we have the right to remain silent or to testify in our own defense, which is the privilege against self-incrimination. We cannot be compelled to testify against ourselves. In the event we elect to remain silent and not testify, we also have the right to not have the jury consider in any way the fact that we elected to remain silent. In our system of criminal justice, a defendant has absolutely no burden to prove that he or she is innocent. It is the government's burden and the government's burden alone to prove the defendant's guilt beyond a reasonable doubt. In effect, the foundation of our criminal justice system might be boiled down to: "You're accusing me? OK then, go on and prove it!"

When I stop and reflect on these rights, I realize quite clearly that my question as to whether a "dashboard case" is the kind of case that "should not go to trial" has a very simple answer: a defendant in a "dashboard case" has the same right to plead not guilty and go to trial as any other defendant accused of a crime in these United States. End of story.

12. Tell the Judge to F*** Off!

Except while interpreting, I cannot speak for anyone but myself. Indeed, when I was interpreting, there were far too many chaotic, brain-boggling moments when I knew beyond a shadow of a doubt that I was not speaking for anyone at all—or at least not speaking for anyone in a coherent or intelligible manner! So, when I say that one of the more memorable and deplorable things about being a court interpreter is that you have to cuss out the judge from time to time, I am speaking in my own voice, and strictly for myself. I should also note for the record that on each and every one of the occasions when I had to swear at a judge out loud, I was, as they say, "engaged in the performance of my official duties."

To begin with, my experience suggests that cussing out the judge is not memorable in a good or rewarding way, but rather in a dramatic way (more on this below). If you ask me, cussing out the judge does not provide some inherent or universal satisfaction in the spirit of that old saying, "Nobody likes a dentist," applied instead to judges. Why? First of all, because there is very little reliable evidence that dentists and judges are equally unlikable. As a matter of fact, different patients and/or defendants clearly seem to dislike one category more than the other. I say this based upon the comparative vehemence with which I have heard people express their dislike for dentists or judges. Second, and more to the point, there are some people who do not dislike dentists or judges at all. These are people who, to the contrary, genuinely like at least a few representatives of both professions. Over the years, for example, I have run into a number of people who claim with convincing sincerity that they "really like Judge So-and-So," and they don't give a hoot what other people say about "that old So-and-So."

No, just because you may not care personally for a judge does not necessarily mean that you would derive a perverse sense of satisfaction from cussing him or her out in the course of interpreting for some foul-mouthed defendant. After all, while serving as an interpreter, you are not cussing the judge out in your own right, nor in your own voice, but rather as the mouthpiece or "bullhorn" of the defendant. Whatever heady rush of personal satisfaction that one might experience from engaging in this sort of indirect, secondhand cussing, would appear to be fleeting and watered down at best.

As suggested above, part of the reason why cussing out the judge is memorable has to do with the inherently theatrical nature of the courtroom setting, along with the high-and-mighty status of the judge in the American justice system. A jury trial is a structured human drama in which the courtroom is the set, each of the participants has a specific role to play, and the ultimate reading of the verdict by the jury can at times be a riveting dramatic climax. As for the judge, along with the dentist, who possibly ranks higher on an imaginary, notoriously fickle, Social Prestige Index (SPI) in America today? Well, first of all, the president and the pope, of course. That goes without saying. Next comes a stellar cluster of larger-than-life movie stars, followed closely by a select group of superstar athletes; prime-time television actors and daytime talk show celebrities; world-famous singers, musicians, writers, artists, comedians, and magicians; a handful of supermodels; rubber-limbed circus acrobats; astounding escape artists; and doctors—maybe. After these come your giants of the corporate arena, tycoons of the financial markets along with a handful of infamous "hired-gun" criminal defense attorneys or traveling snake-oil-salesmen-type figures. Last but not least, there are a few flamboyant, corrupt politicians or lovable scoundrels—those lifelong addicts of the limelight who blow kisses to the cameras and to the few straggling members of their once proud entourages even as they report to prison to begin serving their long-delayed sentences. Only these figures—and not necessarily all of them on any given day—are generally considered more prestigious than the pain-inflicting figure of the dentist or the stereotypically wizened, shrunken-hearted figure of the judge.

When it comes to power, though, judges are in a different league. Unlike most of their more glamorous superiors on the SPI, the legal authority vested in judges endows them with enormous power, which they wield in different ways. One of the most common ways is by issuing judicial orders. For example, in criminal matters, judges can order search warrants. They can order that a person be arrested on a complaint or a bench warrant and be held in custody. They can order that a person be released from custody on bail, dismiss criminal charges against a defendant, rule on legal motions, and decide what evidence may or may not be admitted in evidentiary hearings and trials. Judges can determine the guilt or innocence of the defendant in bench trials. In all cases in which defendants are found guilty, whether by guilty plea or verdict, judges have the power to impose sentence. Depending on the maximum punishment authorized by law for a given offense, judges can impose sentences as severe as life behind bars or even death. Following the imposition of sentence in a given case and depending on the circumstances, judges can also revisit the matter and modify the sentence previously imposed. In cases where attorneys behave in an unprofessional manner, judges have the indescribably delicious power to sanction them. Judges are also authorized to preside over a broad range of civil lawsuits in which they likewise wield enormous legal power.

It is not for nothing that judges wear those sobering black robes, perch like crows from atop and behind those benches big enough for Paul Bunyan, and peer down fiercely on bleating humanity from beneath those jumbo-sized seals of the United States of America. The black robe, elevated bench, American flag, giant seal of the federal government, and scales and/or statue of justice are all outward trappings to create a larger-than-life image of an aloof, eminent personage imbued with enormous power and authority, which is exactly what a judge is. In comparative, auditory terms, whereas the interpreter might be considered to be the cardboard "bullhorn" or plastic "kazoo" of the defendant, the judge might be considered to be the earth-shaking boom box or thundering bass drum of the law itself.

Unfortunately, these traditional, outward trappings of justice may have inadvertently contributed to that unfair stereotype of the judge as a wizened, shrunken-hearted figure. Over the years, I worked in the courtrooms of a substantial number of judges. Based on my experience, I can honestly say that the percentage of judges fitting that stereotype appears to be infinitesimally small or even nonexistent. In fact, I would go so far as to say that most of the judges that I have seen are quite well-hydrated, big-hearted figures—well-intentioned, often heroic figures, who, just like the rest of humanity, are doing their best not to make fools out of themselves against heavily stacked odds. Judges are not infallible. If they do not always successfully administer justice in the course of their daily work, well, who could? I mean, if a baseball player is considered quite successful when he hits safely in approximately three out of every ten at bats, might not the same rule of thumb apply to judges regarding the percentage of time they attain a just result when sentencing defendants for their crimes? Why should society cling to its unattainably high expectations about judges actually doing justice in each and every "at bat?"

Setting such silly business aside, another observation I have made while working in courtrooms is that judges are mortals too, despite the larger-than-life "shadow on the wall," which the imposing courtroom getup contrives to create. In *The Wizard of Oz*, the great and powerful wizard behind the curtain is finally exposed by Dorothy as a silver-tongued, good-hearted traveling salesman whose hot-air balloon was blown far off course one day, and ultimately came to rest in a fantastic land far from Kansas. In like manner, it turns out that judges are not really bigger than life, nor better than everyone else. Not that they are smaller than life, nor worse than everyone else, mind you, just not bigger or better. It also goes without saying that each and every judge is a unique human being. This is another reason why cussing out a judge is invariably a dramatic moment; you never know how he or she is going to react.

I was in court one morning a number of years ago, interpreting for numerous defendants whose cases were set for routine matters including probation revocations, continuances, waivers of indictment, and arraignments on the indictment. For all intents and purposes, it was "another day in the justice factory." Almost all of the defendants were in custody, and all of them were accused of having committed one or more of the routine federal immigration offenses or narcotics offenses that keep the "factory" running at full capacity. Either by handling one or two cases at a time, or by handling larger groups, we had finished running each and every defendant "through the chute" for the morning, except for one. Nobody bothered to tell me ahead of time why they were calling the last defendant's case separately from those of numerous other defendants whose cases were also being continued, but I sort of figured out why afterward.

"Number such-and-such on the calendar," called the clerk, "the United States vs. Jesús Fuentes-Navarro." The marshals went back into the holding cell adjacent to the courtroom to fetch the defendant. I was waiting at the open end of the jury box as the marshals escorted the defendant into the courtroom. They gestured to him to step up into the slightly raised floor of the jury box and stand next to me, which he did.

I said good morning to the defendant as he entered and asked him if he needed an interpreter. He glanced at me and must have made some sort of affirmative response in reply, which would explain why I interpreted for him. The defendant was a Mexican man of medium height, powerfully built, probably somewhere between his late thirties to mid-forties. He stood in the jury box with his arms crossed, glaring across the courtroom at the judge.

"Good morning, Mr. Fuentes," said the judge. I interpreted the judge's greeting to the defendant, to which he did not reply. Then the judge launched into his brief, formal explanation that today was the date and time set for the defendant's preliminary hearing, but that the defendant's lawyer had informed the court that he needed additional time (i.e., a "continuance") to receive the evidence in the case from the government, review it with the defendant, and advise the defendant on how best to proceed in his case. The judge told the defendant that he was willing to grant his attorney's request for additional time, so long as the defendant agreed to the postponement of his preliminary hearing. Finally, the judge asked the defendant if he consented to the continuance as requested by his attorney. As he finished speaking, the judge looked over at the defendant and me.

I finished interpreting the judge's explanation and question into Spanish for the defendant and looked up at him, awaiting his reply.

A longer-than-normal moment ensued, during which the defendant said nothing. Then he turned to me and said in Spanish, *"¡Dígale al juez que chingue a su madre, junto con todos los demás!"* I stared into empty space for a second, looked at the judge, and interpreted the defendant's reply into English as, "Tell the judge to f*** off, along with everybody else!" (Had I wished to literally render the defendant's insult into English, I would have said, "Tell the judge to f*** his mother." I opted instead for the more idiomatic "to f*** off").

There was a split-second pause. What would the judge do or say? The judge, bless his heart, never missed a beat. Unperturbed, he listened calmly to my interpretation of the defendant's profane insult, and said something to the effect of, "All right, Mr. Fuentes, your comment is noted for the record." Then he went about his business, just as though the defendant had replied normally.

In that stressful moment, I was struck by the judge's decency and civility. His ability to focus on the task at hand and not let the insult of a disgruntled defendant get under his skin said a lot to me about the judge's inner calm and self-control. I would not be at all surprised if the judge thought of a couple choice words of his own to reply in kind to the defendant. After all, the judge was human too. Nevertheless, he exercised his good judgment and did nothing of the sort. Just because the defendant had been disrespectful to him did not mean the judge had to lose his temper, give the defendant a piece of his mind, or exercise his judicial prerogative to hold the defendant in contempt of court. Just because the judge had the power to reprimand or crush the defendant did not mean that he had to exercise that power. In the courtroom that morning, the judge was the better man.

It is worth noting that the angry, foul-mouthed defendant, besides speaking rudely to a judge who had addressed him respectfully and who had done absolutely nothing to provoke him, also shielded himself behind the interpreter by using the old "tell the judge" line to do his cussing indirectly, instead of cussing directly at the judge. Maybe the defendant wasn't quite as fearless as he wanted to appear.

Another cussing-in-court incident that comes to mind also took place a number of years ago. It was an incident in which it was not absolutely clear whether the cusser was directing his insult at the judge, at the prosecutor and his agents, or at all of the above. I was in another courtroom at the time, interpreting for a motion hearing in the case of a medium-sized group of Spanish-speaking defendants, all of whom were accused of having conspired to distribute industrial amounts of one illegal drug or another. For security reasons, the marshals had also shepherded these defendants into the jury box. There they stood, listening through their headsets as I interpreted the proceedings for them via some form of the listening equipment that we have used over the years. As is often the case when we process large groups of defendants at the same time, I had not had any time to clearly identify who was who—that is, which of the names listed on the daily court calendar corresponded to which of the defendants who were physically present.

For the most part, the hearing in question had to do with the government's progress in fulfilling its so-called "discovery" obligations to the defendants—that is, the government's obligation to make known and turn over the evidence in the case to the defense. As it happened, it was a case in which the government had wiretapped the defendants' telephone lines and had recorded hundreds if not thousands of telephone conversations between the defendants—conversations in which the defendants had guardedly discussed their illegal narcotics trafficking business. The government had also secretly observed and videotaped the defendants' transactions and recorded their conversations as they engaged in their drug deals with undercover agents as well as other bona fide customers. Given the large number of defendants involved, the lengthy duration of the investigation, the voluminous number of intercepted telephone conversations, and the numerous surveillance reports, videos, and undercover recordings, it was taking the federal prosecutors an unusually long time to turn over all of the government's evidence to the defense attorneys. As a consequence, the defendants—all of whom were in custody—were obliged to wait in jail for a period of several long months in order for their attorneys to finally be in a position to give them sound advice about how to proceed in their cases. Whether one happens to be guilty or not, sitting in jail is not pleasant, and the defendants were understandably not happy about their situation.

One of the prosecutors assigned to the case was giving a very lengthy, detailed update to the judge about why it was taking so long for the government to complete the process of transcription and translation of the wiretapped telephone conversations and other audio recordings in the case. Between the judge's very specific inquiries and the prosecutor's very detailed answers, the update seemed to go on forever. As the prosecutor went along and in reply to the judge's questions, he would repeatedly interrupt his remarks to turn around and confer quietly with one of the case agents about the status of the evidence-preparation process. It was during one of these breaks in the proceedings that one of the male defendants standing closest to me exclaimed in a loud, clear voice, *"¡Hijos de la chingada!"*

I interpreted the defendant's very common Mexican-Spanish expletive out loud into English as "Sons of bitches! Everyone stopped what they were doing and stared curiously at the interpreter standing next to the jury box. The cussing defendant also looked at me uneasily. It occurred to me that he may have cussed out loud for the benefit of his codefendants, and perhaps had not been expecting that his audible remark would be interpreted out loud for the record. I looked back at him. Then the judge asked, "Who said that?"

Because I did not know the defendant's name, I raised my arm and pointed my finger straight at the man who had cussed. The judge looked down at his copy of the court calendar and said, "Let the record show that the interpreter has pointed to defendant Conde-Lemus."

The judge and the prosecutors scurried around for a moment or two, trying diligently to ascertain at precisely whom the defendant had cussed. Meanwhile, as I recall, the cussing defendant's attorney seized the opportunity to sidle over to the jury box and request my traitorous assistance to help him confer with his disgruntled client. The attorney very politely and firmly reminded the defendant that anything he said in court could be used against him, and that things would probably end up going much better for him in the long run if he just kept his f***ing mouth shut. Chastened, the cussing defendant nodded his understanding and assent.

As I recall, the judge and the prosecutors never could decide precisely who the defendant was calling "sons of bitches." As such, none of the likely "cuss-ees" could summon enough moral outrage about the incident to properly berate the "cusser." In the end, the episode of the ambiguous cusser turned out to be just another "tempest in a teapot."

Amid the attorneys' long-winded remarks and the judge's rulings on the motions, the defendant's profane outburst was soon lost and forgotten.

In the end, I do not recommend ever cussing out a judge, any more than I recommend cussing out anybody. However, if by some misfortune you ever find yourself accused of a crime, and you feel that you must cuss out the judge, then I would much prefer that you cuss out the judge "in the first person." That is, have the courage and consideration to cuss the judge out in your own voice, without hiding behind your lawyer or the interpreter. Speak directly to the judge. Say, "F*** Off, Your Honor!" Don't stoop to saying, "Tell the judge to f*** off!"

You see, if you use the old "Tell the judge" line, the problem is that you have no idea of the caliber and temperament of the judge to whom you are speaking in such a flagrantly disrespectful manner. Thankfully, there is an overwhelming majority of keen-witted, perceptive judges who would look over at you cussing at them and see two distinct figures. Those quick-witted judges will immediately realize that the foul-mouthed figure standing over there cussing at them is you—the defendant—not the interpreter, (i.e., your faithful mouthpiece or "bullhorn").

At the same time, there would also appear to be a tiny minority of somewhat less perceptive judges—judges who might look over at you cussing at them and see only one foul-mouthed figure standing there—something akin to an enraged bull incapable of distinguishing between the bullfighter and his maddeningly elusive cape. The next thing you know, both you and the interpreter might be hoisted on the bull's razor-sharp horns, then flung like rag dolls right out of the courtroom and directly into jail. That might not mean much to you as you may already be in custody, but what about the interpreter? After all, you would be the real cusser who should perhaps be held in contempt of court. Why should an innocent court interpreter end up spending a night alongside you in jail, you sorry son-of-a-billy-goat, just for doing his or her job?

13. "I Imported Marijuana?"

Early one afternoon, I went to the marshals' cellblock with a defense attorney to interpret for him and for his Spanish-speaking client. The attorney's client was a female defendant who the attorney would be meeting for the first time. The defendant was already inside the interview room when the attorney and I arrived. She sat on the bench on the other side of the security screen that divided the room, with her arms resting on the counter. Although she wore baggy, jail-issue overalls, she was clearly an attractive woman who looked to be somewhere between her late thirties and early forties.

"Good morning," said her attorney. "Are you María Hernández?"

"Yes, I am," replied the defendant.

"It's nice to meet you," said the attorney, smiling in greeting through the screen.

"It's a pleasure to meet you too," she replied, smiling back at him briefly.

"Mrs. Hernández, this gentleman with me is a court interpreter," the attorney told her. "The interpreter will interpret what you say into English for me, and he will interpret what I say into Spanish for you, OK?"

"Thank you. Nice to meet you," said Mrs. Hernández, looking at me. I nodded and smiled in reply.

"The court has appointed me to represent you, Mrs. Hernández," said the attorney. "We only have a few minutes before we have to go to court, but I wanted to at least meet you briefly, get some information from you, and let you know what I have found out so far about your case."

"Thank you," she replied.

"To begin with," said the attorney, "I have received the complaint in your case, along with one of the reports of the agents who arrested you and questioned you afterward."

"Uh-huh," she replied.

"I also want to tell you," he continued, "that although we are still at a very early stage of your case, I have already received an offer from the prosecutor assigned to your case."

"What kind of an offer?" she asked.

"It is a deal," the attorney replied, "or an agreement we could make with the government—that is, the prosecution—to settle your case. Usually, the faster and sooner we can settle a case, the less time that the defendant—that is you, Mrs. Hernández—will have to serve in jail. In other words, if you accept the government's offer to plead guilty sooner rather than later, the judge in your case will probably give you a shorter sentence, meaning you will be released sooner, and be able to go home to your family sooner."

"Well, the sooner the better, because I don't like being here," she told him.

"Well of course you don't," the attorney replied magnanimously. "Nobody likes being in jail. Well, I shouldn't say 'nobody,' but almost nobody. I have been defending people in these types of cases for over twenty-five years, and in all that time, I have only met a couple of crazy people that liked being in jail. So anyway, you don't have to decide now, of course, but if you are willing to plead guilty to a charge of possession of marijuana—"

"Possession of what?" she asked, evidently taken aback. "Well, supposedly, according to the report of the agent who arrested you, after they advised you of your rights—"

"Mm-hmm. What is that about my rights?" she asked.

"Well," the attorney explained, "the agent's report says that the agent told you that you had a right to be represented by an attorney, and that you had a right to remain silent and not answer his questions without having your lawyer present.

The report says that you waived your right to remain silent, and that you agreed to answer the agent's questions without a lawyer being present."

"Yes, I answered their questions," said the defendant.

"Right," said the attorney. "Anyway, the report goes on to say that you admitted to the agent that you knew that the car in which you crossed the border had marijuana loaded in it, and that you were going to be paid for crossing the car into the United States and delivering it to a parking lot in San Ysidro."

"I imported marijuana?" she asked, with what sounded like real panic in her voice.

The attorney looked at his client through the screen. "Well, Mrs. Hernández," he said, "I am just telling you what the report says that you yourself told the agent. Remember, I wasn't there when you were arrested. Anyway, according to the agent's report, you admitted to the agent that you were being paid to bring the marijuana across into the United States. You told him that you did not know for sure, but that you thought that the car probably had ten or twenty kilograms of marijuana hidden inside, because the smugglers told you that you were going to be paid $1,000 for crossing the car into the United States. According to the agent's report, even though you did not know the exact amount of marijuana that would be hidden in the car, the payment of $1,000 was the same payment that you had been given on the six previous occasions when you had crossed cars loaded with marijuana into the United States, and so you figured that you were probably crossing approximately the same amount each time."

"I crossed marijuana into the United States six times?" Mrs. Hernández asked incredulously.

"Well, according to what the agent says in his report, you actually crossed marijuana into the United States seven times, including this occasion on which you were arrested."

"Seven times? Oh my God!" she exclaimed, and clapped her hand to her forehead in apparent disbelief.

By now, based on the defendant's expressions of shock, panic or incredulity, I was having doubts that the María Hernández who was sitting on the other side of the security screen was the same María Hernández who had been arrested for allegedly smuggling marijuana. I finally decided to pipe up, so I said to the attorney, "Counsel, based on Mrs. Hernández's responses, I am wondering if maybe this is not the right María Hernández."

The attorney nodded at me and said, "I was just thinking the same thing."

Then I asked her, "Mrs. Hernández, are you a witness or a defendant?"

"I am a witness," she replied. "Supposedly the Border Patrol agents want me to testify that I saw the person who put me in the trunk of the car that I was hiding in, but I never saw anybody."

I interpreted Mrs. Hernández's response into English for the attorney. Then I told him, "Counsel, I have a funny feeling that we are interviewing the wrong María Hernández."

"Yeah, me too," he said. "Mrs. Hernández, I am terribly sorry for the confusion, and for frightening you. Please let the guard know that you are a witness, not a defendant, and that I want to talk to the María Hernández who is a defendant—I mean the one who is charged with importation of marijuana."

"I imported marijuana?" she asked again, still in an apparent state of disbelief.

"No, not you, Mrs. Hernández," the attorney answered. "There must be another María Hernández."

"Oh, thank God!" she exclaimed. "I thought you were telling me that I had marijuana in the car in which I was hiding."

"No, no, my mistake," the attorney told her. "I thought you were a different María Hernández."

"Well, my name is María Hernández," she said, "but thank God you were not talking about me. Did the other lady have marijuana?"

"Well, I can't talk to you about that," the attorney said, "because I am her attorney, not yours, and everything that she and I will talk about is confidential."

Mrs. Hernández looked at the attorney through the screen for a moment and asked, "So if you can't talk to me about her case, why are you talking to me? Are you my attorney?"

"No, Mrs. Hernández," he replied, with an increasing tone of exasperation in his voice, "I am not your attorney. I mean, if what you say is true, then I am talking to you by mistake."

"Did I make a mistake?" she asked.

"No, Mrs. Hernández, you did not make a mistake," he replied. "I made a mistake. I thought that you were my client, but if you are a witness and not a defendant, then it is a different María Hernández who is my client, not you."

"Oh, I see," she said. "So, if you are not my attorney, do I have to talk to you?"

"No, Mrs. Hernández, you do not have to talk to me," he told her. "In fact, you should not talk to anybody about your case except your attorney."

"Do I have to talk to my attorney?" she asked.

"Well, nobody can force you to talk to your attorney if you do not want to do so," he told her, "but I would strongly advise you to talk to your attorney, because that is how your attorney finds out about the facts of your case, what you may have seen and heard as a witness, and also whether you have any family members or friends who can help you get released on bail."

"If I talk to my attorney," she asked, "will he ask me about the marijuana that was in the car?"

"Mrs. Hernández, as I understand it, you are a witness, not a defendant," the attorney told her. "You are not being charged or prosecuted for bringing marijuana into the United States, so far as I know. You are being held as a witness in a case of alien smuggling. In other words, someone allegedly brought you into the United States illegally, and the government wants you to testify about how you crossed into the United States, and whether you can identify the person who was driving the car in which you were hidden, and so on."

"So, I wasn't bringing marijuana into the United States?" she asked.

The attorney threw his hands up in exasperation. "How the hell would I— pardon me, Mrs. Hernández," he replied. "How would I know if you were bringing marijuana into the United States?" he asked.

"I am sorry," she told him. "So, was the driver bringing marijuana into the United States?"

"Mrs. Hernández, I haven't any idea who was bringing marijuana and who wasn't bringing marijuana into the United States! Why are you asking me these questions? Don't you understand that I am not your attorney, and you are not my client? You should not be talking to me about your case, and I am not going to ask you anything about your case! Why are you asking me all these questions anyway?"

"Mr. Attorney, forgive me," she replied, "but you *are* asking me about my case, and you say that you are not my attorney. If you are not my attorney, why are you asking me questions?"

The attorney opened his mouth to say something, then thought better of it and closed his mouth. He stared at Mrs. Hernández through the screen.

She stared back at him for a long minute. Then she asked him, "Mr. Attorney, do you have a right to remain silent too?"

"Do I have a right to—Shit!" said the attorney. "I feel dizzy. Officer! Officer!" he called in a loud voice.

After a moment, the detention officer opened the door on Mrs.

Hernández' side of the room, and asked, "What's up, counselor?"

"Would you please take this lady out of here?" the attorney asked. "I think maybe we have a case of mistaken identity. I need to talk to the María Hernández who is going to be arraigned this afternoon on a charge of importation of marijuana. I think this is the wrong person."

"Sorry, counselor," said the officer. "We have no other María Hernández on the court list for today."

"Are you kidding me?" asked the attorney.

"No. Look for yourself," said the officer, holding the court list up to the security screen so that the attorney could see it. "We have nobody else by that name."

"Son-of-a—" the attorney exclaimed. "You mean I have spent all this time talking to the wrong person, only to find out that you don't even have my client on the court list? Hold on a minute. Don't take her away yet. Thanks, officer."

The detention officer left the interview room, closing the door behind him.

"Mrs. Hernández," the attorney asked, "are you sure that you were not arrested for importing marijuana?"

"I was arrested for importing marijuana?" she asked.

"How the hell would I—look, Mrs. Hernández," he told her, "you tell me if you were or were not arrested for importing marijuana into the United States. When you were arrested, didn't they tell you what the charges were?"

"Are you my lawyer?" she asked him.

"No, Mrs. Hernández. I mean, look," the attorney replied, "I'm just asking you if you are the María Hernández who was arrested on suspicion of crossing marijuana into the United States."

"You are not my lawyer?"

"No, goddammit! I'm not your lawyer unless—"

"You told me that I should only talk to my lawyer, and you are not my lawyer," Mrs. Hernández told him. "Should I talk to you or not?" Then she looked at me, the interpreter, and asked me, "Should I talk to him or not?"

I translated her question into English for the attorney.

"Mrs. Hernández, he is the interpreter, not the attorney," the attorney told her. "Please do not ask him for advice. Look, Mrs. Hernández, I am not your lawyer unless you are the same María Hernández who was arrested for importation of marijuana, and who I have been appointed by the court to represent. Do you remember if you were arrested for importing marijuana into the United States?"

"Well, to tell you the truth, the trunk that I was hiding in had a funny smell," she replied.

The attorney glanced at me and whispered knowingly, "It's about time! Finally, we're getting somewhere, eh?" Then he asked Mrs. Hernández, "What do you mean *funny*?"

"Well, I have never seen marijuana or smelled it," she replied, "so I can't be sure, but the trunk that I was riding in had a smell like grass or alfalfa or something."

"Mrs. Hernández," the attorney asked her, "when you came into the United States, were you driving the car or were you hiding in the trunk?"

"Well, at first I was driving," she answered, "because I know how to drive, and I had been asked to drive the car across the border. Then just before we were arrested, the other lady changed her mind and told me to crawl back into the trunk."

"So, Mrs. Hernández," he said, with an unmistakable hint of triumph in his voice, "in fact, you *were* driving the car that had marijuana in it, at least for part of the time?"

"Well, I can't be sure if the car had marijuana in it or not," she said, "because as I say, I have never seen or smelled marijuana before."

The attorney looked down for a moment at the papers he had

spread on the counter before him, his brow furrowed. Then he looked at Mrs. Hernández again. "So, Mrs. Hernández," he asked her, "do you remember if you were driving the car when it crossed the border into the United States, or did you crawl back and hide in the trunk before the car crossed the border?"

"Well," she said, "I remember that the lady told me to crawl back into the trunk when we were very close to the border. I could see the lights of the border crossing and see the men in uniform and the ones that were walking around with the dogs. But I kept driving for a couple of minutes after that until we stopped again in the line of cars. The next time we stopped was when I crawled over the seat and hid inside the trunk."

"Mrs. Hernández," the attorney asked her, "just out of curiosity, do you know if there were any other undocumented people who were also riding in the car besides you?"

"Yes, there were several other people who were also hiding in the trunk," she replied. "I know because I bumped something with my head, and someone said "ouch" when I crawled back into the trunk. But since it was dark, I couldn't see what or who I had bumped with my head."

"Mrs. Hernández, was the voice that said 'ouch' a man's voice or a woman's voice?" asked the attorney.

"I don't know," she answered. "It was very dark in the trunk, and I couldn't see anything."

"Mrs. Hernández," he asked, "do you know if there were any other ladies named María Hernández in the car that you were driving and hiding in?"

"Well, I heard a couple of the other ladies say that their name was María," she said, "and I also remember that two or three of the other people had the last name Hernández, but I don't know for sure if any of those Marías were Hernández, or if any of those Hernándezes were Marías."

Then he said, "Mrs. Hernández, how many people were riding in the car that you were driving and hiding in?"

"I saw eight or ten people when the officers took us out of the car at the border inspection," she replied.

"And do you know how many of them were held in custody as witnesses, just like you, and how many of them were released and sent back to Mexico?" he asked.

"The agents kept two or three of the women in custody with me," she answered, "and I don't know how many men, because they put them in different cells. They also kept two of the men as witnesses, and the rest of the people were sent back to Mexico."

"Mrs. Hernández, please try to think and remember," the attorney said. "When the agents had all of you get out of the car, did they search the car?"

"Yes," she replied. "They brought a dog, and the dog jumped inside the trunk and started scratching. Then the agents started taking things out of the trunk."

"Did you see what kinds of things the agents were taking out?" he asked.

"Well, like plastic bags and backpacks, and some small suitcases," she replied. "I think some of the people were bringing clothes with them."

"Mrs. Hernández, did you have any belongings with you in the car?" the attorney asked.

"Just a backpack with some clothes inside it," she told him.

"Mrs. Hernández," he asked, "did you have anything else with you?"

"Well, one of the other ladies said that I had a small pink suitcase with me when I got into the car, but that is a lie," she said. "I had never seen that pink suitcase before the agents took it out of the car and asked whose it was."

"Did the suitcase have a name tag on it?"

"Well," she replied, "the agents were asking all of the ladies what our names were, and if any of us were named María Hernández."

"Mrs. Hernández, what did you tell them?" the attorney asked.

"I told them that my name is María Hernández," she answered, "but that I had never seen that suitcase before. What is more, the name on the name tag was María Hernándes-Lópes, spelled with an "s" at the end of "Hernándes" and "Lópes," and I am Hernández-López spelled with a "z" at the end of Hernández and López."

"Mrs. Hernández, did you ever find out what was inside that pink suitcase?" he asked.

"Well, supposedly the agents found some other drug called 'crystal' or amphetamine or something," she replied.

"Mrs. Hernández, do you know if the agents arrested anyone for importing methamphetamine into the United States?" the attorney asked.

"Supposedly, they were going to arrest one of the Marías for importing the marijuana and one of the other ladies for importing the methamphetamine," she answered, "and one of the other ladies for bringing the illegal people into the United States, but I don't know which one was which."

"Mrs. Hernández," the attorney asked, "are you saying that someone who was with you in the car was arrested for importation of marijuana into the United States?"

"I imagine so," she answered, "but since I have never seen or smelled marijuana before, I can't be sure that is what the agents found, or if they arrested one person for importing the marijuana and another person for importing the crystal, or if they just arrested the same person for importing both drugs and someone else for bringing in the illegal people."

"Mrs. Hernández, are you sure that you are a material witness, and that you have not been arrested for importing marijuana, or maybe arrested for importing methamphetamine or maybe arrested for smuggling aliens into the United States?" the attorney asked.

"Mr. Attorney," she replied, "are you my attorney?"

"Mrs. Hernández, I don't know if I am your attorney or not!" he answered.

"Mr. Attorney," she said, "if you don't know if you are my attorney or not, why are you asking me all of these questions?"

"Mrs. Hernández, I am asking you all of these questions because I am trying to find out if you are the María Hernández who has been charged with importation of marijuana, and who the court has appointed me to represent. And I would appreciate it if you would stop asking me questions when I ask you questions, and just answer my questions. I am the attorney, and you are the defendant who has been accused of committing a crime—I mean, you might be the defendant who has been accused of importing marijuana, and therefore you might be my client. That is what I am trying to find out, and that is why I am asking you these questions."

Mrs. Hernández stared at the attorney for another long minute. She appeared to be thinking. The attorney stared back at her through the security screen. The minute of silence dragged on and on. Finally, Mrs. Hernández broke the ice.

"Mr. Attorney, are you going to keep asking me questions, or are you going to remain silent?" she asked.

"Mrs. Hernández, I'm not the one who is accused of a crime at the moment, so I don't have any reason to remain silent!" he told her, his voice rising almost to a shout. "I am a criminal defense attorney, for God's sake! Why would I want to remain silent if I have done nothing wrong?"

"Well, I haven't done anything wrong either," she told him, "and even so, I still want to remain silent."

"Mrs. Hernández, why do you want to remain silent if you are a witness and not a defendant?" the attorney asked her.

"Because if I am a defendant, I have a right to remain silent, and if I am a witness then you are not my attorney," she replied.

"But Mrs. Hernández—" he began.

"Mr. Interpreter," she said, addressing me.

"Yes, ma'am," I replied.

"Please tell this attorney that he has a right to remain silent and not ask me any more questions, just like I have a right not to answer any questions until my attorney is present," said Mrs. Hernández, "and please tell him not to ask me any further questions until I find out for sure if he is my attorney or not. Until then, I will remain silent."

I gleefully interpreted Mrs. Hernández's requests into English for the attorney. Once again, the attorney opened his mouth as if to speak. Then he evidently decided to heed his "client's" cockeyed advice. He looked down at the floor, shoulders slumped in defeat. Then he put his papers back in his briefcase, closed it, and slowly stood up.

"You win," he said wearily. "I can't take it anymore. Good luck, Mrs. Hernández, whatever you are, and whoever your attorney is. Maybe I'll see you again once I get some more information. If not, good-bye, ma'am."

"Thank you, Mr. Attorney," she replied. "Good luck to you too," she added earnestly.

He turned and opened the door to leave the room. At that instant, the other door opened, and the detention officer poked his head inside the room, gesturing to Mrs. Hernández to accompany him.

"Hey, counselor," he said. "We just got word that a group of defendants and witnesses got booked into Metropolitan Correctional Center a little while ago. Two of the females are also booked under the name of María Hernández. Actually, one of them is listed as Hernández-López, and the other one is listed as López-Hernández. We have already made the jail run for today, so those people will be put on the court list for tomorrow morning. Also, the duty prosecutor in arraignments court just told us that at first this female that you have been interviewing was going to be a defendant. Then they decided to keep her as a witness, and now they are thinking of charging her again. Come with me, ma'am." he said, gesturing to Mrs. Hernández.

The attorney stared at the detention officer and asked, "Officer, do you have the names of those people who just got booked into MCC written down, by chance?

"Yes, sir, I've got them right here," replied the detention officer, holding up a sheet of paper.

"Can you tell me how those other detainees named María Hernández-López spell their last names? I mean, with a "z" or an "s" at the end?" the attorney asked.

The detention officer looked closely at the names on his sheet of paper. He shook his head and replied, "It's hard to tell. It looks like the name of the lady booked under 'Hernández-López' has Hernándes spelled with an "s" at the end and López spelled with a "z" at the end. The other lady's name has López spelled with an "s" at the end and Hernández spelled with a "z" at the end. To be honest with you, this is a photocopy of a computer printout from the jail, and the "s" and the "z" look a lot alike. You also gotta remember that sometimes the arresting agents don't know Spanish very well, and they mess up the spelling of the detainees' names."

"Yeah, thanks a lot, officer," the attorney said, and held the interview room door open for me. As we walked down the hallway to leave the cellblock, the attorney muttered darkly under his breath. Then he turned to me and said, "Now I've seen everything. A defendant who advises her lawyer to remain silent, and not ask her any more questions. How the hell am I supposed to explain this to the judge? Oh well, if he asks me why I am not prepared to proceed, I guess I'll just tell him that there was a mix-up in the cellblock, and as a result, I have not been able to verify that the lady I was interviewing is in fact my client. I'm sure that will just tickle the judge to death."

"Well, counsel, tomorrow is another day, right?" I offered hopefully.

"Yeah, tomorrow is another day," he said.

By this time, the attorney and I had ridden the elevator together from the basement up one level to the ground floor of the courthouse. As the doors opened and we began to go our separate ways, I couldn't resist the urge to give the attorney two cents' worth of gratuitous advice. Smiling happily at him I said, "Don't forget, counsel, if the judge starts asking you about why you are not prepared to proceed, just advise him that under the Fifth Amendment to the Constitution, you have a right to remain silent and not answer any incriminating questions, and that His Honor also has a right to remain silent and not ask you any more incriminating questions until he knows for certain that you are the attorney who is representing Mrs. Hernández."

"Yeah, right," replied the attorney. "Everybody and their uncle have a right to remain silent—even the judge, the pope, and the goddamn man in the moon. Thanks for your help in the tank, and for your brilliant legal advice, wise ass." We both burst out laughing. Then he turned, shook his head, and trudged resignedly toward the courtroom

14. Court Suggestion Box

In all the years I have worked in the courts, I have yet to see a suggestion box affixed to the outside of the courtroom door or screwed to the end of the jury box or bolted into either side of the podium or glued to the side of the witness stand or nailed right smack dab in the middle of the judge's bench. This is a shame, because although many people like to boast that the United States has the best justice system in the world, it clearly has plenty of room for improvement. There could be a label on the box with writing to the following effect: "Got an idea for how to improve your justice system? Please place your suggestion in the box. Thank you for caring, your friendly Court Improvement Suggestion Committee."

Of course, whenever you give the public the chance to make suggestions, you are likely to get some sensible, thoughtful, constructive suggestions, and you are also likely to get some impractical, foolish, even nonsensical suggestions. The job of periodically collecting, duly considering, and ultimately recommending to the judges whether to discard or implement the suggestions would be the job of a friendly Court Improvement Suggestion Committee. If you were lucky or unlucky enough to be on the Suggestion Committee, what would you make of the following suggestions?

The Guiltometer - An astonishingly simple, surprisingly economical measuring device to assist the jury and/or court in quickly and effectively determining the guilt or innocence of defendants in jury trials or bench trials. Imagine a device something along the lines of a lie detector but fine-tuned and infinitely more reliable. The guiltometer would have a series of wire sensors and/or probes that would be comfortably and inconspicuously attached to a defendant's head and body. The wires would be connected to a guiltometer processing unit, which in turn would be connected to a very large, round-faced dial with an enormous indicator needle, much like a clock or a large water pressure gauge. The dial would have a series of marks that would gradually change from black to red, corresponding to the degree of the defendant's innocence or guilt. Large letters such as "UI" for "unmistakably innocent" would correspond to the black marks at the low end of the scale, while large letters such as "HG" for "hopelessly guilty" would correspond to the red zone at the high end of the scale. The dial would be situated in such a way that the court and jury could see the needle throughout the entire trial. Neither of the lawyers would ever be able to see the needle during the trial. The purpose of not letting the lawyers see the guiltometer would be to keep them from sticking their foot in their mouths, and improperly swaying the jury. For example, a sneaky prosecutor could not snatch a cheap victory by stooping to spontaneous utterances such as: "My God, ladies and gentlemen of the jury, this defendant just broke the guiltometer!" Nor could the defense attorney argue disingenuously to the jury that if the prosecutor has nothing to hide, why isn't he hooked up to the guiltometer also? The guiltometer needle would be a wonderfully responsive pointer. If a defendant were unmistakably innocent, a jury would see the guiltometer needle nestling peacefully in the black zone at all times, even during the most furious onslaughts of the prosecution's case. On the other hand, if a defendant were hopelessly guilty, the jury would see the needle leap straight up into the red zone, and constantly tick violently against the very top mark, as though straining to zoom straight off the dial. There it would remain throughout the trial, like a damning, accusatory finger pointing straight at the defendant's unmitigated guilt. Of course, a number of pesky hurdles remain to be surpassed before you get a guiltometer going like gangbusters in every courtroom in America, but just think of the possibilities!

The Prevaricating Witness Ejector Seat - Everyone agrees in principle that there is no place for lying in a court of law. Lying makes a mockery of the solemn oath that every witness swears or affirms to testify truthfully and to not bear false witness. Lying also plays hell with the idea that the search for justice is a search for the truth. You cannot do justice unless you first seek the truth, except perhaps by mistake, accident, or hapless bumbling. That being said, the number of witnesses who violate their oath and perjure themselves with utter abandon is absolutely staggering. Over the years, while engaged in the performance of my official duties as a court interpreter, it is possible that I may have achieved the dubious distinction of having uttered more lies than any human being throughout recorded history. If I never did quite attain that opprobrious niche in some deplorable *Book of Infamous World Records,* there is no doubt in my mind that I was well on my way. Whether they are crooks or cops, they should not lie in a court of law, but they do. So, what might an indignant judge or jury do to abruptly put an end to the situation when a witness has finally, ignominiously gone far beyond the bounds of anything remotely resembling the truth? What about the idea of a "Prevaricating Witness Ejector Seat?" I'm not exactly sure what the quantitative or qualitative criteria for summary ejection should be, probably some sort of cumulative threshold. The supporting technology could perhaps be calibrated on a scale of one to ten, where one represents truthfulness, while a mendacity reading in the neighborhood of six or seven gets you ejected through a sliding glass opening in the roof. Whatever the particulars, I feel strongly that the judge's bench and the jury box should both be equipped with ejector buttons. For that matter, what about the attorney who called the witness in the first place? Why should the attorney have to sit on his or her hands and listen to a pack of lies? I know that if I were serving as a juror in a trial, I would feel a sudden rush of appreciation and attribute a greatly enhanced sense of credibility to that honest, dedicated, advocate-turned-ejector. One ticklish question might be whether witnesses should be duly warned or specifically admonished about the possibility of ejection, or should they not be warned, and "let the witness beware?" If the Suggestion Committee thinks it would be appropriate to admonish witnesses, it would be as easy as pie to recommend a simple modification to the oath administered to witnesses. Consider the following slightly modified version of the oath: "Do you solemnly swear or affirm with full knowledge of the penalties for perjury—including summary ejection from the witness stand—that the evidence you are about to give in the cause now before the court will be the truth, the whole truth, and nothing but the truth, so help you God?" Finally, for purposes of dramatizing solemn, judicial omnipotence as well as deterring other prospective prevaricators who may still remain within earshot, what about the idea of adding some prerecorded, sonic-boom-like sound effects at the moment of ejection?

The Chute of Doom - This is not my suggestion. I got it from my younger brother, who listened to my suggestion about the ejector seat, and decided to do me one better. The chute of doom is the downward-tilting answer to the upward-catapulting ejector seat. Both suggestions are intended to make short work of witnesses who lie through their teeth on the witness stand. The difference would be as follows: in the aforementioned ejector-seat scenario, the witness would find himself or herself being abruptly shot from the witness chair through the opened roof of the courtroom and out into the wild blue yonder, only to land in a circus-style safety net situated on the roof of the courthouse. From there the marshals would lead the ejected witness directly downstairs to the basement for booking. By contrast, in the courtroom equipped with the chute of doom, the lying witness would stare down aghast at an opening that gradually opens wider and wider beneath his or her squirming feet. The more the witness lies, the larger yawns the opening, until finally there is no floor left underneath the witness stand. Suddenly, the witness chair tilts forward, and the witness whooshes haplessly down the chute of doom, lies and all, coming to rest in the marshal's office for immediate booking. No sonic-boom-like sound effect would accompany the downward-sliding liar. If anything, perhaps a recording of a high-pitched, quickly stifled cry as the chute opening instantly slams shut in preparation for the next heedless prevaricator. Like the ejector seat, the matter of who gets to pull the lever to set the chute of doom in motion would naturally be subject to exhaustive review and consideration. What about the idea of the courtroom bailiffs also having a say in the matter and a hand on the lever? Of course, there are many who believe—and perhaps rightly so—that law enforcement personnel would be far too inclined to "chute first and ask questions later."

About the Author

Matthew Mendenhall worked as a federally certified court interpreter in the U.S. District Courts in San Diego, California, from 1985 until he retired in 2010. Before that, he taught Spanish-language courses for three years as a Lecturer at North Carolina State University in Raleigh, North Carolina, where he met and married his wife, Lynn Little. He has a Graduate Certificate in Spanish-English Translation-Interpretation and an MA in Hispanic Literature, both from UC Santa Barbara. He and Lynn live in San Diego, CA. They have two wonderful daughters and two grand dogs.

Acknowledgement

In high school, Mr. Bramblett was the unfailingly cheerful teacher of our watered-down Introduction to Chemistry class. On those occasions when I would make another fine mess of a lab experiment, Mr. Bramblett would shake his head patiently, smile kindly and say, "Mr. Mendenhall, bumpkin technique!" The class turned out to be fascinating, and I've never forgotten Mr. Bramblett.

Given how long it has taken to get *Adventures in the Justice Factory* to its current state, it is now painfully clear that even in high school, Mr. Bramblett saw in me the unmistakable mark of a congenital practitioner of bumpkin technique.

For this reason, I wish to acknowledge my editor Valerie Brooks at www.TheWriteEdit.com for her two invaluable rounds of painstaking editing and detailed notes. For your honest, insightful feedback, and for your encouragement and suggestions, thank you Valerie! Thanks to you, the manuscript now seems exponentially less infested with bumpkin technique.

Of course, just as it is nearly impossible to pull every single weed out of a garden, so it seems almost impossible to entirely eliminate bumpkin technique from a manuscript. In the end, an objective, thorough editor can only do so much. As the proverb says, "You can lead a horse to water, but you can't make it drink." All weeds that have still not been eradicated from *Adventures in the Justice Factory* are my responsibility and mine alone.

Matthew Mendenhall

Books by this Author

"Like curios left on a dusty shelf…." *Curios: Poems and Prose* is comprised of selected poems and prose that the author has written and revisited repeatedly over the last five decades. These small pieces of language have become keepsakes of the people, places, and moments that they memorialize. The effort to make and improve them continues to be one of the most rewarding experiences of a lifetime. But how delightful it would be if other people were to read and enjoy them too! Hence, the decision to publish this collection of curios after so many years. *Curios* is available in Kindle Edition, paperback, and hardcover at Amazon.com.

Made in the USA
Monee, IL
05 November 2026

67386142R00100